MEGATRENDS

The Transformative Forces Reshaping the United States

M. JAKE AGUAS

PRELIMINARY EDITION

Kendall Hunt
publishing company

Cover image © Shutterstock.com

www.kendallhunt.com
Send all inquiries to:
4050 Westmark Drive
Dubuque, IA 52004-1840

Published in the United States of America

To Shelli Lynn—The little things that you have done to help those around you have changed more lives than you could possibly imagine. Your mom is so proud of you.

To Austin Jacob and Ashley Rae—You bring joy to my life each and every day. You are right where you need to be.

To my parents, Mario and Lucy—You love and give endlessly. Vero and I could never thank you enough for all you have done for us.

Contents

Acknowledgments

My gratitude on this project goes out to many people who have directly or indirectly contributed to the development of Megatrends: The Transformative Forces Shaping the United States. First, I would like to acknowledge my copyeditor, Ken Gërhart, for his partnership and world-class effort on this project. I would also like to thank Marques Jessie and his talented team at Kendall Hunt Publishing (David Tart, Angela Lampe, and Megan Drake) for their unwavering support and commitment to the book's success.

I recognize and acknowledge the following for their influence and inspiration:

Mentors Bill Brooks, Andy Carney, Shaun McDougall, Dr. Chuck Prince, and Chuck Pillsbury for investing in me, challenging me, and helping me to see not just what is, but what could be.

Colleagues and leaders in the banking and financial services industries:

Jamie Dimon, Henry Walker, Pablo Sanchez, Mike Weinbach, Ryan McInerney, Charlie Scharf, Scott Powell, Tasunda Brown Duckett, Jerry Towe, Mike Reed, Dan Deegan, Nikki Hartung, Michael D'Aisilio, Connie Gieger, Michelle Kurranty, Anthony Chan, Terri Decker, Kim Bera, Jennifer Hewes, David Schilling, Linda Goldsmith, Lawrence Bailey, Edgar David, George Kaye, Scott Kipers, Dr. Betty Uribe, Sonja Kehnt, Marc Shay, Brian Dahlquist, Paul Kiner, Juan Cano, Brian Giles, Marcy Hasegawa, Anthony Cua, Edna Hallrud, Ken Schroeder, Kyle Gomez, and Caren Sanchez.

Biola University and the Crowell School of Business:

Dr. Gary Lindblad, Dr. Barry Corey, Dr. Deborah Taylor, Dr. Rick Bee, Connie Salios, Dr. Richard Franklin, Dr. Jeff Decker, Drs. David and Jill Bedell, Ron Smedley, Dr. David Bourgeois, Dr. Lari Mobley, Dr. Dave Keehn, Dr. Shelly Cunningham, Dr. Rick Langer, Dr. Andre Stephens, Michael Pierce, Lee Wilhite, Brian Miller, Brenda Velasco, Adam Morris, David Shynn, Brian Shook, Jackie Beatty, Dr. Todd Pickett, Dr. Scott Rae, Dr. Nick Sherwin, Dr. Jeff McHugh, Dr. Thomas Wilson, Dr. Steven Rundle, Laureen Mgrdichian, Les Harmon III, Helen Mitchell, Andrea Marrero, Shane Enete, Philip Woodward, Dr. Brandon Ware, Dr. Wlamir Xavier, Dr. Randy Markley, Beth Starr, Paul Sohn, Robert Curtis, Dr. Robert Harp, Jordan Terranova, Dr. John Tuttle, Lillian Minar, Miki Gao, Kayley Allen, Joseph Cruz, Madeleine Prater, Dr. Christina Kim, Dr. Carrie Stockton, Dr. Sean McDowell, Dr. J. P. Moreland, Jasmyn Alvarez, Tiffany Lee, Dr. Walter Augustine III, Tamra Malone, Lester Larios, Norlan Hernandez,

Alicia Miller Andre, John Stupar, Gordon Hummel, Tessa Steele, Andrew Yee, Tim Milosch, Joseph Rubio, Matthew Weathers, Matthew Hodges, Lavonue Scannell, Dr. Dave Grant, and the Biola University Human Resources Team.

Chapman University and the George L. Argyros School of Business and Economics: Dr. Daniele Struppa, Dr. Tom Turk, Dr. Candice Ybarra, Dr. Raymond Sfeir, Director Mario Leone and the Leatherby Center for Entrepreneurship and Business Ethics, Rob Ryan, Jennifer Brady, Karen Akiyama, Marshall Toplansky, Eric Jaegers, Kyle Mackie, Nicci Julian, Luke Rider, Dr. Cristina Giannantonio, Dr. Mark Maier, Stacey Moynahan, and Eva Valencia.

The Regent University School of Business & Leadership PhD Program:

Dr. Bruce Winston, Dr. Doris Gomez, Dr. Debra Dean, Dr. David Winner, Dr. Joshua Henson, Dr. Maurice Buford, Dr. Mihai Bocarnea, Dr. Kathleen Patterson, and Dr. Andy Wood.

Rick Warren, Fred Martin, Robert Mayer, Morgan Cey, Morris Interactive, Dean West and the Orange County Department of Education, Stanley Chen and Jeremywell International, Peter Beshai, Sara Robinson, Filip Smagorowicz, Christopher Ames, Scott Pauker, Alexander Brown, Mark Merriles, Stephen Christensen, Janet Muller, George Wright, Ashlie Andrews; Adolfo, Veronica, Sienna, Geneva, and Bentley Gomez; Sandra, Dennis, and Grace Calderon; Elaine and Jesse Alvarado; Angie, Alfredo, and Giselle Ponce; Walter, Eddie, and Renatto Aguas; Kylo Ren Aguas and Queen Nalah Amidala Aguas.

About the Author

Jake Aguas is a GenExpert and Associate Professor of Management in the Crowell School of Business at Biola University and a Clinical Professor of Management at the Argyros School of Business and Economics at Chapman University, where he teaches management, leadership, human resources, and entrepreneurship at the MBA and undergraduate levels. Jake has co-led international study tours to Beijing and Shanghai, China, and Hong Kong, instructing on culture, behavior, and economics in modern China. He has also worked on philanthropic projects in the United Kingdom, South Africa, and Central America.

Jake is an organizational consultant and practices internationally, helping leaders build stronger organizations through their people and processes. Jake specializes in leadership strategy, team building, training and development, coaching, and the design and implementation of global human resource management functions.

Jake has held leadership positions with Fortune 100 companies in financial services as well as in the market research industry with one of the country's top polling firms. He was a leader in the retail bank division of JPMorgan Chase for 15 years, notably serving as its Human Resource Manager for Talent Acquisition for the Western United States. In addition to authoring publications for research and professional journals, he regularly speaks on leadership, generational differences, emotional and cultural intelligence, and entrepreneurship.

At the University of California, Los Angeles (UCLA), Jake studied under Nobel Prize laureate, Lloyd Shapley, and economists William Allen, Armen Alchian, and George Hilton, which shaped and influenced his economic and entrepreneurial approaches to management. Jake is bilingual in Spanish and English and pursuing a PhD in Organizational Leadership from Regent University. He holds a master's degree in Organizational Leadership from Biola University and a bachelor's degree in Economics from UCLA.

Jake is the author of numerous professional and research journal articles including "Generation Z: The Rise of a New Generation" and "The American Working Woman: A Century in Review." In addition to *Megatrends: The Transformative Forces Reshaping the United States*, Jake is co-authoring *Generation Z and the COVID-19 Crisis*, forthcoming from Kendall Hunt Publishing.

Chapter 1

Introduction to Megatrends

metamorworks/Shutterstock.com

The world continues to change, and the global environment continues to react to a group of large-scale forces that are reshaping the values, ideals, attitudes, and psychosocial constructs of its population. These trends are transforming the way people live their lives here in the United States. According to a leading business consulting firm, megatrends are defined as "transformative, global forces that define the future world with their far-reaching impacts on businesses, economies, societies, cultures and personal lives" (Frost & Sullivan, 2014, 2019). Simply put, megatrends are a group of macroinfluential pressures that stimulate and demand responses from the inhabitants

> **Megatrends:** The transformative forces that define the future world with their far-reaching impacts on businesses, economies, societies, cultures, and personal lives.

of a given population. David (2004) describes the unfolding of these types of simultaneous occurrences and system-wide developments in economics, demography, and technology as composite scenarios of smaller-scale patterns.

These megatrend forces flow across industries and sectors with fluidity—they do not discriminate. They affect science and art, politics and law, education and innovation, and entertainment and agriculture. From the farmer to retailer, leader to the follower, the preschooler to the professor emeritus, the residents of the seniors club in Rowland Heights to the guests of the Burj Al Arab (the only "seven-star hotel" in the world), no one is immune to the prompting of megatrends. The United States has been a leader in advancing the global megatrend movement through its hunger for continuous innovation, its increasing focus on sustainability, and its reaction to a dynamic and changing population composition.

mohamed alwerdany/Shutterstock.com

The Burj Al Arab hotel in Dubai during a New Year's event.

In preparing to explore the significant impact that these megatrends are having on the constructs of management, organizational behavior, human resources, entrepreneurship, and similar subjects, it is essential first to take a step back and view the global diorama. By examining the significant forces that are currently impacting the global landscape, stakeholders begin developing a well-rounded perspective of "the why" behind the unique differences that influence motivation and behavior. This is particularly important to younger generations seeking purpose and significance in the workplace as well as in their personal lives.

Generation Z and Millennials seek purpose and significance.

There are numerous benefits to wrestling with megatrends. First, the comprehension of these Goliath movements increases a leader's acumen and influential reach by providing him or her with a relevant knowledge base from which to make well-educated decisions that consider both macro- and microlevel perspectives. Often, leaders suffer from ethnocentrism, the tendency to place their own group at the center of their observations, preventing them from fully understanding differing viewpoints (Moodian, 2009; Northouse, 2019). As a result, the effectiveness of their analysis and decision-making processes become compromised. A study of megatrends encourages an ethnorelative mindset, which encourages

> **Ethnocentrism:** The tendency to place one's group at the center of their observations, often preventing them from fully understanding differing viewpoints.

respect and consideration of the many values and behaviors that come with an openness to learn from the "bigger picture," a challenge to step out and "play" outside the comfort zone if you will.

Second, a study of megatrends creates a multidisciplinary lens through which to observe the world. While investigating the cause and effect of the world's events, one is exposed to a wide array of subjects, such as leadership, philosophy, entrepreneurship, health, environmental science, money, and travel—to name a few. Scrutinizing events from numerous angles provides clarity and opens the field of view, introducing us to a new spectrum of colors—we don't know what we don't know until it's brought to our attention. Allow me to illustrate this thought through a personal experience. In my undergraduate studies, I remember sitting in the back of a lecture hall for a course in microeconomics. My vision was generally good at the beginning of my first 10-week term (UCLA operates under the quarter system), but it gradually began to give in to "fuzziness" as the term progressed. The good news was that it seemed to reset itself each term, so I thought nothing of it. However, one term was particularly different. As the quarter progressed, the grease boards and monitors continued to become blurrier and seemed to stay that way into the next term. One of my colleagues noticed I was squinting continuously and recommended that I see an eye doctor. I strongly resisted since I thought the view was normal for everyone from this distance. I finally gave in one day and decided to see an optometrist. As it turned out, I had a respectable astigmatism. Remember that I had not acted earlier because "I did not know what I did not know." I'll never forget trying on my first pair of corrective contact lenses. In an instant, I began seeing the world in an entirely new fashion. Not only could I clearly see the board from the back of a 450-seat auditorium, but I could also now see subtle color variations and details in the vegetation around campus. I could see people's facial expressions and read their body language. Even reading became more enjoyable as I did not have to bounce my reading material back and forth in order to gain focus. The point is that corrective lenses and glasses changed the way I observed, processed, learned, and reacted to events happening around me. Learning megatrends will do the same for your business, leadership, and management acumen.

As a relentless student of megatrends, you will gain access to the subtleties, nuances, and the varying shades that exist within the management, entrepreneurship, human resource, organizational behavior, and leadership spectrum. As a result, your **emotional intelligence (EQ)**

> **Emotional Intelligence (EQ):** The capability of individuals to recognize their own emotions and those of others, discern between different feelings and label them appropriately, use emotional information to guide thinking and behavior, and manage and/or adjust emotions to adapt to environments or achieve one's goal(s). Goleman (1995, 1998)

cla78/Shutterstock.com

and social intelligence (SQ) will also improve (more on that later) and you will become better equipped to navigate life's situations and challenges more effectively. This becomes helpful when interacting with people that you may have less in common with, such as individuals from different cultures, genders, industries, and generational cohort groups.

> Social Intelligence (SQ): An aggregate measure of self and social awareness that influences one's capacity to negotiate complex social change (Ganaie & Mudasir, 2015), commonly referred to as "tact," "common sense," or "street smarts" (Riggio, 2014).

Finally—and perhaps the most significant value-add—an understanding of megatrends can elevate your level of confidence, conviction, and compassion, which in turn allows you to be more impactful in both your personal and professional life. I was blessed by inspiring mentors in my retail banking and financial services careers, and each one shaped and refined me in a different fashion. Bill Brooks, Andy Carney, Shaun McDougall, and Nikki Hartung were all senior banking executives and mentors of mine at JPMorgan Chase. What separated them from other outstanding leaders was their ability to demonstrate what I call "humble confidence." They understood what was happening around them—both domestically and globally, and they genuinely invested and poured themselves into their teams, getting to know each member personally and gaining "buy-in" along the way. They were self-assured, confident, and laser focused in their messaging and execution when it was time to *pull the trigger*. They naturally kept themselves well informed and abreast of the megatrends by reading, watching the news, asking a lot of questions, and interacting constantly with employees, partners, and customers alike. It is no surprise that their careers continue to flourish.

Team members debriefing a project with their mentor.

Individuals who are politically, economically, socially, and technologically (PEST) savvy understand how the megatrend forces embedded within the macrolandscape operate as well as how they influence events and situations at a local and micro level. Fortunately, this is a skill that can be learned with commitment and discipline. Individuals who keep up with the megatrends are able to leverage high-level global nuances to make effective granular decisions with precision.

Would you like to be more effective in connecting and leading in your relationships and career? Would having a 30,000-foot view of your landscape—a helicopter ride above the trees, help provide you with more menu options for your decision-making process and interactions? Would increasing the spectrum of colors and detail in which you see the world and your relationships provide an added boost of confidence as you navigate through challenging terrain and rough waters? Then this book is for you.

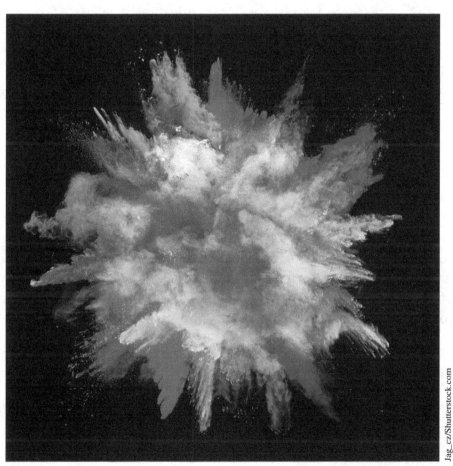

Jag_cz/Shutterstock.com

sdecoret/Shutterstock.com

Discussion Questions

1. Survey those around you and conduct some online research on the construct of megatrends. Based on what you discover, define megatrends in your own words (2 to 3 sentences). Why do you believe that to be the best definition? Specifically describe how you came to that conclusion (process, sources, etc.).

2. How might your understanding and application of megatrends help you improve your personal and professional career? Provide two (2) specific examples.

3. Are there similarities and differences between *megatrends* and *metatrends*? If so, how might you explain this difference to a colleague or work associate? Can you provide an example of each?

4. Think of an individual who has demonstrated the ability to use megatrend thinking at home or in the workplace? How were they able to effectively apply such broad perspectives to solve specific challenges?

5. Without reading ahead, can you guess what a few of the megatrends might be? What specific reasons lead you to think that?

References

David, P. S. (2004). Five meta-trends changing the world. *The Futurist, 38*(4), 22–27.

Frost & Sullivan. (2014). *World's Top Global Mega Trends to 2025 and Implications to Business, Society, and Culture: Macro to Micro Implications of Mega Trends for the World*. Retrieved from https://www.smeportal.sg/content/dam/smeportal/resources/Business-Intelligence/Trends/Global%20Mega%20Trends_Executive%20Summary_FROST%20%26%20SULLIVAN.pdf

Frost & Sullivan. (2019). *Mega Trends: Defining Our Future*. Retrieved from https://ww2.frost.com/consulting/key-client-issues/mega-trends/

Goleman, D. (1995). *Emotional intelligence*. Bantam.

Goleman, D. (1998). *Working with emotional intelligence*. Bantam Books.

Moodian, M. A. (2009). *Contemporary leadership and cultural competence: Exploring the cross-cultural dynamics within organizations*. Thousand Oaks, CA: Sage.

Northouse, P. G. (2019). *Leadership: Theory and practice* (8th ed.). Thousand Oaks, CA: Sage.

Riggio, R. E. (2014). What is social intelligence? Why does it matter? *Psychology Today*. Retrieved from https://www.psychologytoday.com/us/blog/cutting-edge-leadership/201407/what-is-social-intelligence-why-does-it-matter

Chapter 2

Foundations

As we begin exploring the shaping of megatrends in the United States and observing the impressions they are leaving on its population, a meaningful discussion regarding some foundational metrics are in order. Remember that megatrends are impacting the global community at large. However, for the purpose of our investigation, we are directing our attention toward their impact domestically with tangential references to the global environment. If we are to learn about the forces influencing the United States, we need to first understand the audience affected—the US population.

Covering approximately 3.8 million square miles and stretching 2,680 miles horizontally—1,582 vertically—the United States shares borders with Canada

Denali Mountain Peak (Mt. McKinley)

The salt flats in Badwater Basin, Death Valley National Park.

and Mexico and maritime borders with Russia, Cuba, and the Bahamas. Ranked as one of the world's largest countries behind Russia and Canada, 93% of its territory is comprised of land area while 7% is occupied by water. The nation's highest point is Denali (Mount McKinley) in Alaska towering at 20,320 feet, and its lowest point is the Badwater Basin located in California's Death Valley at 282 feet below sea level—the country's average elevation is 2,512 feet (WorldAtlas, 2016).

The average annual temperature in the contiguous United States in 2019 was 52.68°F approximately 0.66 degrees higher than the 20th century average (Wang, 2020). Figure 2.1 shows the average annual temperature of the United States over the past 125 years.

FIGURE 2.1

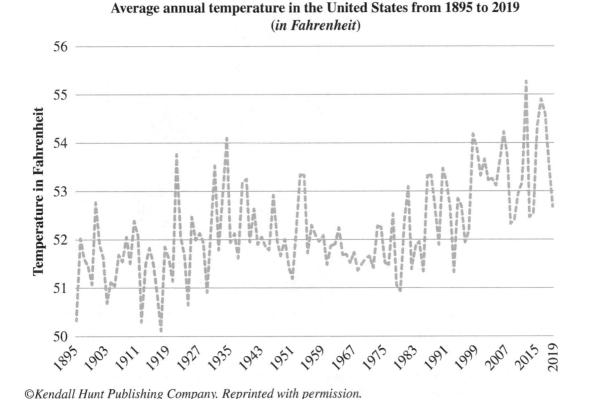

Average annual temperature in the United States from 1895 to 2019
(*in Fahrenheit*)

According to the National Climate Report released in 2019, precipitation in 2018 reached 34.63 inches, a figure 4.69 inches above the long-term average primarily due to the relentless low-elevation rains and heavy mountain snows (National Oceanic and Atmospheric Administration, 2019; Samenow, 2019). These events led the United States to experience its wettest meteorological winter on record during the period from December 2018 to February 2019 (see Figure 2.2)

FIGURE 2.2

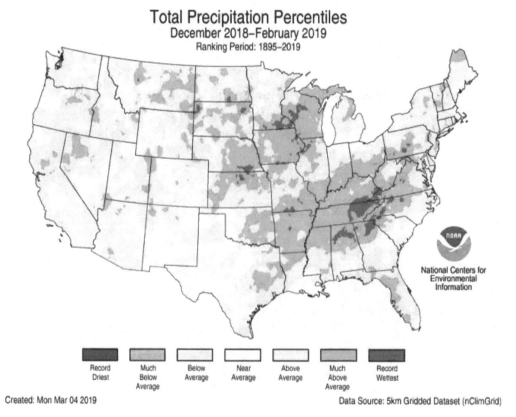

Created: Mon Mar 04 2019   Data Source: 5km Gridded Dataset (nClimGrid)

Precipitation differences from normal over the winter months of December, January and February. (NOAA)

Source: National Centers for Environmental Information, National Oceanic and Atmospheric Administration (NOAA).

According to the United States Census Bureau (USCB), the population of the United States is estimated to be slightly over 328 million (328,239,523) as of July 1, 2019 (USCB, 2019a) making it the third most populated country in the world behind China (1.43 billion) and India (1.36 billion) (World Population Review, 2019). More recent monthly population estimates using a short-term projection methodology place the US population estimate closer to 330 million as of December 2019 (USCB, 2018a). The male to female ratio runs 49.2% to 50.8% respectively, and military veterans make up 5.7% of the current living population (18,611,432). Whites represent 76.5% of the population, Whites that are Non-Hispanic/Latino 60.4%, Hispanics/Latinos 18.3%, Black/African Americans 13.4%, and Asians 5.9%. In a future chapter, we will discuss how the diversity in ethnic composition of the US population is prompting attention at home and in the workplace as more languages, traditions, religious preferences, and cultures are interacting and blending together.

The United States consists of 119,739,128 households containing an average of 2.63 people per household and 21.5%, or about 1 in 5 households, that speak another language other than English at home. The average number of children per family is 1.93 as compared to 2.33 in 1965—a family is defined as a group of two people or more (one of whom is the householder) related by birth, marriage, or adoption and residing together (Duffin, 2020a). The country's median income is $60,293, and 11.8% of its population currently falls below the poverty threshold. In 2017, the poverty rate was 13.4% which indicated a 1.6% improvement from 2017 to 2018 (Benson & Bishaw, 2019)—however, there is still considerable work for policymakers and community stakeholders to do about this co-related construct of poverty and hunger in the United States.

Educational attainment refers to the highest level of education that an individual has completed. Education provides the skills, training, and knowledge necessary to enter a desired profession, advance within that profession, or change career paths altogether. Education

> **Educational Attainment:** The highest level of education that an individual has completed.

assists in career preparation, provides economic and health benefits, promotes personal development (e.g., emotional intelligence, critical thinking, etc.), and exposes learners to areas that may ignite a previously unexplored passion (LaTour, n.d.). Over 87% (87.7%) of the US population 25 years or older has a high school diploma, and 31.5% have a bachelor's degree or higher. The table below highlights the distribution of educational attainment of the US population, 25 years of age and older (see Table 2.1).

TABLE 2.1 Educational Attainment of the Population 25 Years and Over, by Selected Characteristics: 2018 (Numbers in Thousands. Civilian noninstitutionalized population.[1])

Both sexes	Total	Educational attainment								
		None–8th grade	9th–11th grade	High school graduate	Some college, no degree	Associate's degree	Bachelor's degree	Master's degree	Professional degree	Doctoral degree
Total	219,830	8,729	13,682	62,685	35,442	22,369	48,235	21,048	3,172	4,468
		3.97%	6.22%	28.52%	16.12%	10.18%	21.94%	9.57%	1.44%	2.03%
Marital Status										

Source: The United States Census Bureau (2019b).

Overall, the percentages of young adults with high school diplomas, some college, a bachelor's degree or higher have all risen over the last 50 years. In fact, the number of young adults getting bachelor's degrees or higher has more than doubled from 17% to 36% (see Figure 2.3) in the same timeframe. This increase is also consistent for non-Hispanic Whites, Black/African Americans, and Hispanics/Latinos. About half of Asians (51%) 25 and older have a bachelor's degree or higher, compared to 30% of all Americans of this age (Lopez, Ruiz, & Patten, 2017).

Asians represent 5.9% of the US population; however, they make up over 20% of Ivy League students (Tran, Lee, & Huang, 2019). Park (2019) found that Asian Americans are more likely to enroll in highly selective universities regardless of their economic background as they have "more access to resources like higher-quality public schools, supplemental educational resources (e.g., SAT prep), and communities that reinforce high, and arguably rigid, standards for performance" (p. 1). Park (2019) also indicated that Asians may, at times, also benefit from a phenomenon called "stereotype lift" where educators provide a "boost" in evaluations and scores of Asian students based on the notion that Asians are expected to perform well when compared to other ethnic or denigrated outgroups. Walton and Cohen's (2003) work on "stereotype lifts" is an excellent resource for those interested in considering a "deeper dive" on the subject.

FIGURE 2.3

Percentage of Young Adults, Ages 25 to 29, With At Least a High School Diploma, With At Least Some College, and With At Least a Bachelor's Degree: 1971-2017

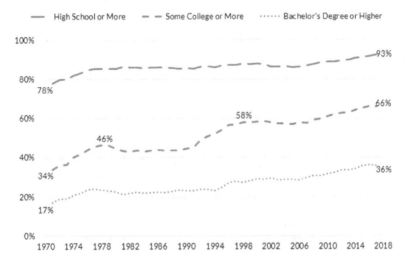

Source: Data for 1971-2001: U.S. Department of Education, National Center for Education Statistics. (2002). The Condition of Education 2002 (NCES 2002–025) [Tables 25-1, 25-2, & 25-3]. Washington, DC: Author. Retrieved from https://nces.ed.gov/pubsearch/pubsinfo.asp?pubid=2002025. Data for 2002-2017: Child Trends' calculations using U.S. Census Bureau. (2003-2018). Educational Attainment in the United States: Detailed Tables [Table 1]. Retrieved from https://www.census.gov/data/tables/2017/demo/education-attainment/cps-detailed-tables.html.

In regard to the topic of gender diversity, it is relevant to consider that the number of females currently receiving bachelor's, master's, and doctoral degrees is exceeding that of their male counterparts (Northouse, 2019). In both 2017 and 2018, the Association of American Medical Colleges (2018) reported there had been more female matriculants in US Medical Schools than men, a paradigm shift that has carried over into the workplace (see Figure 2.4). Today, we witness the impact of female influence and presence in the workplace as positions that have historically been given to men in mid-level management, professional coaching, and academic researchers are going to females that are just as qualified.

FIGURE 2.4 Academic Years 1980–1981 through 2018–2019

The graph below displays the number of matriculants to United States medical schools by sex academic year 1980–1981 through 2018–2019. Matriculants who declined to report sex are only reflected in the "All Matriculants" counts.

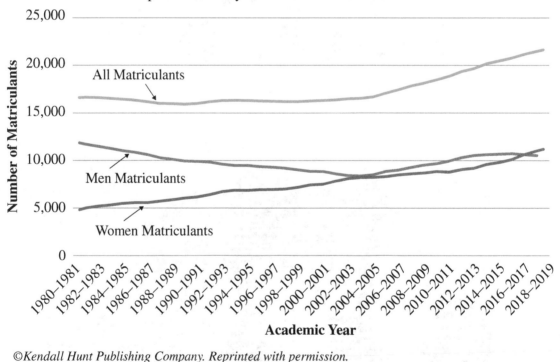

New York, Los Angeles, and Chicago make up the top three of the largest populated cities in the country (see Table 2.2). Nevada and Idaho led the nation by growing more than 2% while Utah, Arizona, and Florida followed with at least 1.5% in annual growth.

TABLE 2.2 The 10 Largest Cities in the United States by Population 2020.

Rank	City	State	2020 Population	2020 Population Density	Area (mi²)
1	New York	New York	8,622,357	28,741/mi²	300
2	Los Angeles	California	4,085,014	8,710/mi²	469
3	Chicago	Illinois	2,670,406	11,764/mi²	227
4	Houston	Texas	2,378,146	3,733/mi²	637
5	Phoenix	Arizona	1,743,469	3,366/mi²	518
6	San Antonio	Texas	1,590,402	3,450/mi²	461
7	Philadelphia	Pennsylvania	1,579,504	11,787/mi²	134
8	San Diego	California	1,469,490	4,521/mi²	325
9	Dallas	Texas	1,400,337	4,119/mi²	340
10	San Jose	California	1,036,242	5,821/mi²	178

©Kendall Hunt Publishing Company. Reprinted with permission.

Irvine, California experienced the highest population growth of any US city (3.87%) while St. Louis, Missouri, experienced a negative growth rate (−1.11%). **Population density** is defined as the number of people living in a per unit area; the United States, New York, San Francisco, and Jersey City rank among the most densely populated cities (see Table 2.3) while Anchorage Alaska, Augusta and Macon-Bibb County in Georgia have the least amount of people per square mile. On average, the population density of the United States runs about 87.4 people per square mile—population density impacts transportation, infrastructure, and the standard of living for its residents.

> **Population Density:** The number of people living in an area. (e.g., people residing per square mile of land).

TABLE 2.3 The 10 Cities with the Highest Populated Density in the United States

Rank	City	State	2020 Population	2020 Population Density	Area (mi²)
1	New York	New York	8,622,357	28,741/mi²	300
2	San Francisco	California	906,419	19,286/mi²	47
3	Jersey City	New Jersey	265,288	17,686/mi²	15
4	Paterson	New Jersey	146,892	16,321/mi²	9
5	Boston	Massachusetts	701,984	14,625/mi²	48
6	Miami	Florida	504,439	14,012/mi²	36
7	Santa Ana	California	335,009	12,408/mi²	27
8	Washington DC	District of Columbia	724,342	11,874/mi²	61
9	Newark	New Jersey	284,420	11,851/mi²	24
10	Philadelphia	Pennsylvania	1,579,006	11,784/mi²	134

©Kendall Hunt Publishing Company. Reprinted with permission.

The United States continues to experience a decline in its annual population growth rate as year-over-year percentages of deaths are exceeding those of births. While the current annual population growth rate is hovering between 0.62% and 0.72%, the rate is projected to continue falling to 0.39% by 2047 (USCB, 2018b) (see Figure 2.5).

In 2018, the United States experienced its first fractional increase in the life expectancy rate in 4 years (Adamy, 2020). Data provided by Murphy et al. (2018) at the Centers for Disease Control and Prevention had indicated that the previous decrease in the life expectancy rate had been contributing to a reduction in the annual **population growth rate**.

> **Population Growth Rate:** The change in population over a unit time period expressed as a percentage of the number of individuals in the population at the beginning of that period.

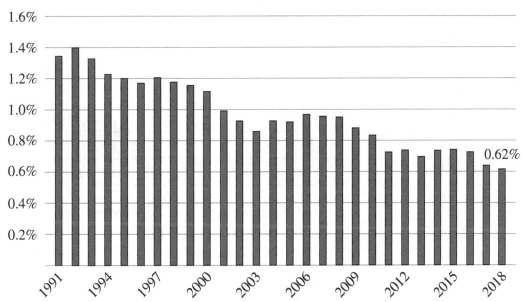

FIGURE 2.5 United States Annual Population Growth 1990–2018

Note: Year shown represents the preceding 12 month period ending July 1.

©Kendall Hunt Publishing Company. Reprinted with permission.

In the United States, the life expectancy rate is approximately 78.7 years–76.2 years for males and 81.2 years for females, a 0.1% increase in both based on the prior year's data (Xu, Murphy, Kochanek, & Arias, 2020). The life expectancy rate is defined as the average number of years of life (from birth) and

> **Life Expectancy:** The average number of years a person is expected to live (average life span) from birth.

serves as a data point depicting the overall health of a nation. In terms of gender, the life expectancy for males has now stabilized after a consistent year-over-year decline that started in 2014 and ended in 2017 while that of females has remained relatively unchanged since 2010 (Kochanek, Anderson, & Arias, 2020) (see Table 2.4).

An interesting data point is that the global life expectancy rate has been moving in the opposite direction. While the life expectancy rate domestically has generally

TABLE 2.4 Life expectancy at birth, by sex: United States, 2010–2018

Year	Total	Male	Female
2010	78.7	76.2	81.0
2011	78.7	76.3	81.1
2012	78.8	76.4	81.2
2013	78.8	76.4	81.2
2014	78.9	76.5	81.3
2015	78.7	76.3	81.1
2016	78.7	76.2	81.1
2017	78.6	76.1	81.1
2018	78.7	76.2	81.2

trended downward over the last few years, the global life expectancy growth rate has continued to rise at a rate of 0.34% per year (World Health Organization, 2018). It would be interesting to conduct a longitudinal study measuring the impact that this developing trend will have on the United States as the needs of the national and global environment shift. The unexpected death toll caused by the recent COVID-19 global pandemic will also provide a rich framework from which to study life expectancy and annual growth rates.

Consider the following questions:

- What effects will the increasing rate of foreign populations have on the United States? On immigration and emigration?
- Will the United States experience a significant increase in the number of immigrants authorized to work on temporary worker visas? What industries are most likely to be affected?
- Will the country's increased investment in STEM education and fluency better position its residents to be globally competitive candidates for opportunities abroad? How so?

From 2016 to 2018 the life expectancy rate had been most impacted by the rising **rates of suicides** and drug overdoses which directly contributed to a decrease in the average life span of the nation's population, a decline not experienced since World War I and the 1918 influenza pandemic (Solly, 2018). The age-specific death rate of 15- to 24-year-olds dropped 5.1% from

> **Suicide Rate:** Death caused by self-directed injurious behavior with intent to die as a result of the behavior (National Institute of Mental Health, 2019)

2017 to 2018—a respectable shift from a 7.8% increase from 2015 to 2016. However, the cohort experiencing the heaviest increase in the percentage of deaths in recent years was that of 25- to 44-year-olds which significantly skewed mortality data (Murphy et al., 2018). Specifically, from 2015 to 2016, 25- to 34-year-olds experienced a 10.5% increase in age-specific deaths, and 35-to 44-year-olds experienced a 6.7% increase (Kochanek, Murphy, Xu, & Arias, 2017). The trend slowed in acceleration from 2016 to 2017, but continued north as the rates for 25- to 34-year-olds increased 2.9% and those of 35- to 44-year-olds increased 1.6%. From 2017 to 2018, all age groups experienced a decrease in the adjusted death rates (Xu et al., 2020).

According to Saiidi (2019), the national suicide rate has increased by 33% since 1999—2015 to 2017 alone experienced a 5.2% climb. Consistent with more recent trends, 2018 suicide rates have stabilized with little change compared to 2017 levels (Xu et al., 2020). On the other end of the spectrum, the global suicide rate has declined by 30% since 2000 with Russia, Japan, and India experiencing the most significant declines. Suicide ranks second as the leading cause of death for 10- to 34-year-olds and the fourth leading cause of death for 35- to 54-year-olds in the United States behind **unintentional injuries**, malignant neoplasms, and heart disease (see Table 2.5).

> **Unintentional Injuries:** Unplanned injuries resulting from events such as motor vehicle crashes, falls, fires and burns, poisoning, aspiration, and drowning.

The ratio of male to female suicide rates has decreased from 4.4% (2000) to 3.6% (2016), reflecting the acceleration in female suicide deaths compared to that of males since 2007 (Hedegaard, Curtin, & Warner, 2018).

According to the American Foundation for Suicide Prevention (2019), about half (50.7%) of the suicide deaths in 2017 were firearms related, while 27.7% came from suffocation, and 13.9% from poisoning—military veterans experience suicide at a rate that is 1.5 times higher than nonveterans.

TABLE 2.5

10 Leading Causes of Death by Age Group, United States – 2018

Rank	<1	1-4	5-9	10-14	15-24	25-34	35-44	45-54	55-64	65+	Total
1	Congenital Anomalies 4,473	Unintentional Injury 1,226	Unintentional Injury 734	Unintentional Injury 692	Unintentional Injury 12,044	Unintentional Injury 24,614	Unintentional Injury 22,667	Malignant Neoplasms 37,301	Malignant Neoplasms 113,947	Heart Disease 526,509	Heart Disease 655,381
2	Short Gestation 3,679	Congenital Anomalies 384	Malignant Neoplasms 393	Suicide 595	Suicide 6,211	Suicide 8,020	Malignant Neoplasms 10,640	Heart Disease 32,220	Heart Disease 81,042	Malignant Neoplasms 431,102	Malignant Neoplasms 599,274
3	Maternal Pregnancy Comp. 1,358	Homicide 353	Congenital Anomalies 201	Malignant Neoplasms 450	Homicide 4,607	Homicide 5,234	Heart Disease 10,532	Unintentional Injury 23,056	Unintentional Injury 23,693	Chronic Low. Respiratory Disease 135,560	Unintentional Injury 167,127
4	SIDS 1,334	Malignant Neoplasms 326	Homicide 121	Congenital Anomalies 172	Malignant Neoplasms 1,371	Malignant Neoplasms 3,684	Suicide 7,521	Suicide 8,345	Chronic Low. Respiratory Disease 18,804	Cerebrovascular 127,244	Chronic Low. Respiratory Disease 159,486
5	Unintentional Injury 1,168	Influenza & Pneumonia 122	Influenza & Pneumonia 71	Homicide 168	Heart Disease 905	Heart Disease 3,561	Homicide 3,304	Liver Disease 8,157	Diabetes Mellitus 14,941	Alzheimer's Disease 120,658	Cerebrovascular 147,810
6	Placenta Cord. Membranes 724	Heart Disease 115	Chronic Low. Respiratory Disease 68	Heart Disease 101	Congenital Anomalies 354	Liver Disease 1,008	Liver Disease 3,108	Diabetes Mellitus 6,414	Liver Disease 13,945	Diabetes Mellitus 60,182	Alzheimer's Disease 122,019
7	Bacterial Sepsis 579	Perinatal Period 62	Heart Disease 68	Chronic Low Respiratory Disease 64	Diabetes Mellitus 246	Diabetes Mellitus 837	Diabetes Mellitus 2,282	Cerebrovascular 5,128	Cerebrovascular 12,789	Unintentional Injury 57,213	Diabetes Mellitus 84,946
8	Circulatory System Disease 428	Septicemia 54	Cerebrovascular 34	Cerebrovascular 54	Influenza & Pneumonia 200	Cerebrovascular 567	Cerebrovascular 1,704	Chronic Low. Respiratory Disease 3,807	Suicide 8,540	Influenza & Pneumonia 48,888	Influenza & Pneumonia 59,120
9	Respiratory Distress 390	Chronic Low. Respiratory Disease 50	Septicemia 34	Influenza & Pneumonia 51	Chronic Low. Respiratory Disease 165	HIV 482	Influenza & Pneumonia 956	Septicemia 2,380	Septicemia 5,956	Nephritis 42,232	Nephritis 51,386
10	Neonatal Hemorrhage 375	Cerebrovascular 43	Benign Neoplasms 19	Benign Neoplasms 30	Complicated Pregnancy 151	Influenza & Pneumonia 457	Septicemia 829	Influenza & Pneumonia 2,339	Influenza & Pneumonia 5,858	Parkinson's Disease 32,988	Suicide 48,344

Data Source: National Vital Statistics System, National Center for Health Statistics, CDC.
Produced by: National Center for Injury Prevention and Control, CDC using WISQARS™.

Centers for Disease Control and Prevention
National Center for Injury Prevention and Control

Source: CDC.

In 2017, 70,237 deaths resulted from drug overdoses—47,600 involved opioids comprising 67.8% of all drug overdose–related deaths. Synthetic opioid–involved overdose death rates increased by 45.2% from 2016 to 2017 (Scholl, Seth, Mbabazi, Wilson, & Baldwin, 2019). No age group, sex, ethnic/racial background, or country urbanization level was immune to the escalating death rate from drug overdoses in the United States. The highest synthetic opioid-involved overdose death rates in 2017 occurred in West Virginia (37.4 per 100,000), Ohio (32.4), and New Hampshire (30.4) while Arizona (122%), North Carolina (113%), and Oregon (91%) had the largest relative year-over-year increases (Scholl et al., 2019).

The amount of opioids prescribed per person is three times higher today than it was in 1999. Opioid prescribing is higher in small cities and large towns, in areas where there are higher percentages of white residents, where more uninsured or unemployed reside, and in areas where people live with diabetes, arthritis, and disabilities. It goes without saying that areas that house more medical professionals such as dentists and primary care physicians also have higher levels of opioid prescribing. Knowing that higher opioid prescribing places patients at risk for addiction and overdose, federal and state governments, as well as healthcare providers are implementing initiatives to help reduce the number of prescriptions, lower dosages, and decrease the number of days that prescriptions are taken. These efforts may be paying off as new data indicates that overdose deaths are leveling off or decreasing slightly (Xu et al., 2020). Results also show that prescriptions have declined from 81.2 per 100 persons to 58.7 around the country (Scholl et al., 2019).

A factor that may have a considerable impact on the future growth rate is the aging Baby-Boomer population (born between 1946 and 1964), which is paving the way for a historic increase in the number of deaths anticipated each year. Baby-Boomer deaths will increase the death count by over one million in 2037 compared to the number of fatalities experienced in 2015 (Devine, 2017). Figure 2.6 illustrates

---

FIGURE 2.6

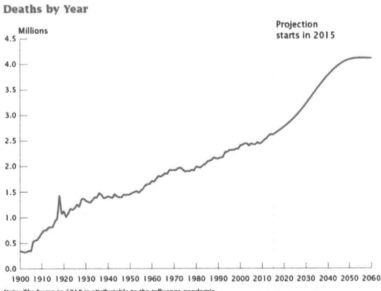

Deaths by Year

Note: The bump in 1918 is attributable to the influenza pandemic.
Source: Centers for Disease Control and Prevention, National Center for Health Statistics (1900-2014) and U.S. Census Bureau, 2014 National Population Projections (2015-2060).

a long-term trajectory suggesting that the death count and percentage of people dying will continue increasing annually through 2050 before beginning to level off.

Younger generational cohorts made up of Millennials and Generation Z are postponing births and marriage, influencing the population growth rate as well. Marriage rates have been on a 30-year decline (Duffin, 2020b) and have fallen in the United States to 6.5 per 1,000 people of population, a decrease from 1990 levels of 9.8 marriages per 1,000 people (see Figure 2.7).

Economist Zagorsky (2016) found that there are 2.5 million fewer marriage ceremonies performed in the United States today when compared to its highest annual peak in the early 1980s. While theorists do not all agree on one specific reason for this trend, fingers are pointing toward rising student debt and housing costs, increasing levels of education and income for women, the fall in religious and faith-based adherence, and the increasing popularity of cohabitation.

FIGURE 2.7

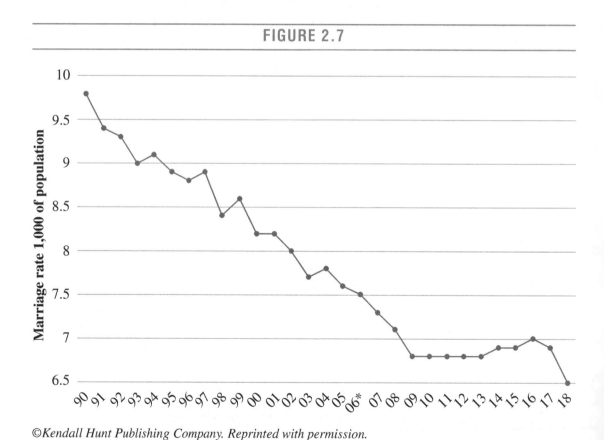

Let me share a story. I once attended a conference where I ran into two individuals that had been cohabitating for 2 years and learned an interesting perspective on their transactional view of marriage. As I was making my way through the business center of the hotel, I passed what looked like an executive strategy meeting—complete with charts and tables drawn up on grease boards. The couple was deep in heated debate, banter, and throwing out marriage statistics as if they were in the middle of defending a research dissertation—it was tense. At first, I did not know what they had been discussing; however, their passionate discussion piqued my interest so I popped in and asked what they were working on. They invited me to have a seat and watch the discussion—something tells me that this was not their first time having this conversation. While one individual crunched numbers on an Excel spreadsheet, the other had just finished a pro versus con marriage T-chart on one board and had started on a financial cost–benefit analysis overlaid with a T-chart on the other board. I took a seat and just observed. When it was over 3 hours later, one smiled at the other and casually said "Well, the numbers don't work out for marriage or children; we will run the numbers again next year and see what they say." They looked at each other agreeably, smiled, hugged, and then went off to have dinner before heading home. Now, that's not to say that all couples take this approach, but it is an example of the mindset that an increasing number of younger generation couples have been taking toward marriage and children that directly contributes to decreasing marriage and population growth rates. The demographic stagnation in the population growth rate has led to declining births in the nation's younger population. According to Frey (2018), the "nation's under 18 population has declined by about 780,000 or 1% and, as a result, the impact is suggesting a long-term trajectory that will yield fewer births as the US population ages with fewer women (proportionately) in their childbearing years."

Even though the net immigration rate—the international migration of both native and foreign-born populations into the United States—is adding over one million documented inhabitants per year (and plans to for the next 20 years), this increased dependency as a contributor to growth is still not enough to make a significant dent or curb the population growth rate. It will be interesting to see how **immigration** policy will impact the growth rate in the aftermath of the COVID-19 global pandemic.

> **Immigration:** The action of coming to live permanently in a foreign country.

The **civilian labor force** in the United States is defined as all persons 16 years of age or older (who are not institutionalized or on active duty) and are either working for pay or actively seeking paid employment (Schiller & Gebhardt, 2017). This statistic does not include the jobless who are not looking for work or discouraged workers who would like a job but have given up looking for employment. In essence, it

> **Civilian Labor Force:** All persons 16 years of age or older (who are not institutionalized or on active duty) that are either working for pay or actively seeking employment.

represents the total number of workers that are available, willing, and have recently sought work. According to reports by the U.S. Bureau of Labor Statistics (2020a), as of December 2019, the current civilian labor force in the United States was comprised of approximately 165 million people. Toossi (2015) projects an average annual increase of 0.5% in the labor force through 2024, a rate slightly less than the previous 10 years (2004 to 2014). The **labor force participation rate** (those employed and actively looking for work divided by the total civilian noninstitutionalized population) hovered around 62.7% in March 2020 (McMahon, 2020). The United States had been experiencing a declining and historic 50-year

> **Labor Force Participation Rate:** The Labor force as a percent of the civilian noninstitutional population.

low in the seasonally adjusted **unemployment rate** (see Figures 2.8 to 2.10), which had fallen as low as 3.5% (Davidson, 2019). April and May 2020 reports from the U.S. Bureau of Labor Statistics (2020b, 2020c) indicated that the unemployment rate had increased from 10.3% to 14.7% after more than 33.5 million Americans—a proxy for job loss—had sought unemployment aid due to the effects of the coronavirus (COVID-19) pandemic on the labor market, both as a result of the illness and efforts to contain the virus. I encourage you to study the varying forms of unemployment that exist (structural, cyclical, frictional, seasonal, regional, voluntary, etc.) and challenge you to develop a deeper understanding of the employment climate in the United States.

> **Unemployment Rate:** The number of unemployed people (16 years or older, available to work full-time in the past four weeks, actively looking for work in the past 4 weeks, and temporarily laid off) divided by the total number of people in the civilian labor force.

FIGURE 2.8 Civilian Unemployment Rate, Seasonally Adjusted

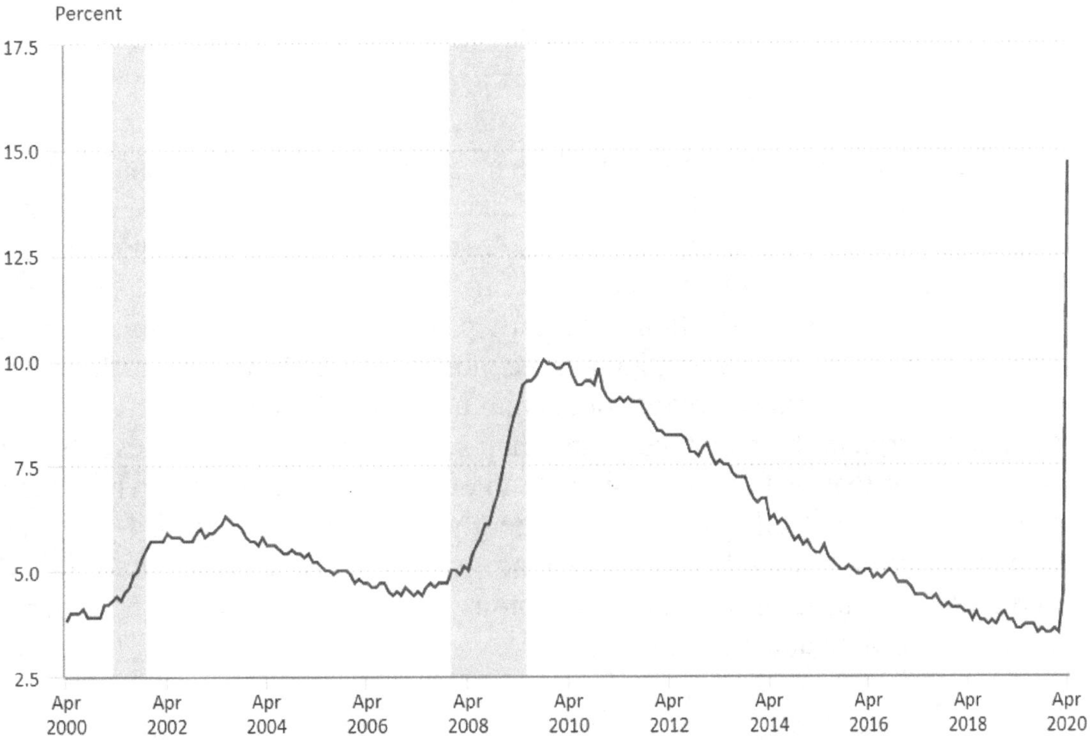

Source: U.S. Bureau of Labor Statistics.

FIGURE 2.9

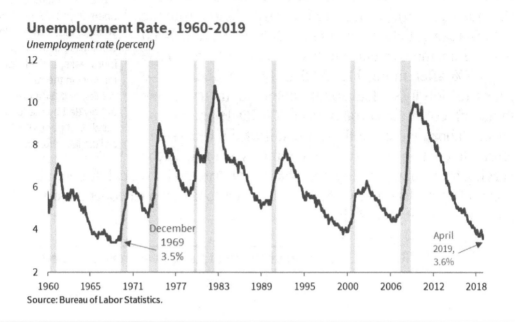

Unemployment Rate, 1960-2019

Unemployment rate (percent)

December 1969 3.5%

April 2019, 3.6%

Source: Bureau of Labor Statistics.

Whether you are reading this book as a resource for your organization or as a text for a graduate course, developing a fundamental understanding of economics and demography and their relationship to megatrends will help you on your journey regardless of your career or calling. Entrepreneurs, parents, executives, community leaders, production assistants, pastors, schoolmates, athletic teams, farmers, and brick masons all make economic-based decisions in their daily routines. The more you increase your economic understanding, the better you will be able to explain the megatrends and their relationships to current events—and to history for that matter. You'll be able to effectively discuss the "why" behind financial and cyclical patterns, confidently articulate the impact of events domestically and globally, provide sound guidance to peers and direct reports, and manage your own personal situation as you determine when and where to commit your time and resources.

FIGURE 2.10 130 Years of Unemployment Rates in the United States

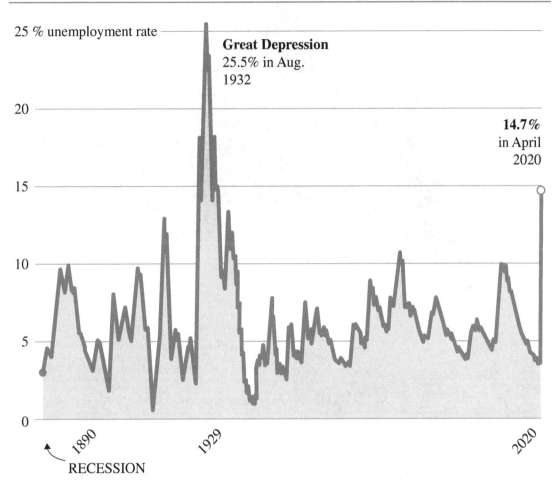

©*Kendall Hunt Publishing Company. Reprinted with permission.*

Arthimedes/Shutterstock.com

Discussion Questions

1. How might the slowing population growth and decreasing life expectancy rates in the United States impact the workforce and job opportunities domestically and abroad? Are there specific industries and/or countries that will be more impacted than others? Explain.

2. Conduct research on suicide and drug overdose levels in the United States. What are currently the top three causes? What trends do you see? Are the rates increasing, leveling off, or declining? What solutions might you propose to help improve the situation?

3. Identify two countries outside the United States with increasing life expectancy rates. Discuss the reasons why the countries' rates are increasing. How specifically do they differ in comparison to the United States?

4. Go to www.census.gov and conduct a search on population statistics in the United States. Identify three (3) demographic statistics about the population that have not been discussed in the chapter. Explain each and discuss what you learned from the data?

5. What are the differences between structural, cyclical, frictional, seasonal, regional, and voluntary unemployment? Provide a specific example of each.

References

Adamy, J. (2020, January 30). Life expectancy rises in U.S. for first time in four years. *The Wall Street Journal.* Retrieved from https://www.wsj.com/articles/life-expectancy-rises-in-u-s-for-first-time-in-four-years-11580398277

Association of American Medical Colleges. (2018, December). *2018 applicant and matriculant data tables.* Retrieved from https://aamc-black.global.ssl.fastly.net/production/media/filer_public/92/94/92946165-0060-4376-9736-18c89688efd0/applicant_and_matriculant_data_tables.pdf

Benson, C., & Bishaw, A. (2019, November). Poverty: 2017 and 2018. *The U.S. Department of Commerce, U.S. Census Bureau.* Retrieved from https://www.census.gov/content/dam/Census/library/publications/2019/acs/acsbr18-02.pdf

Davidson, P. (2019, October 4). Employers added 136K jobs in September while unemployment rate hits a new 50-year low. *USA Today.* Retrieved from https://www.whitehouse.gov/articles/unemployment-rate-falls-lowest-level-nearly-50-years-u-s-economy-adds-263000-new-jobs-april/

Devine, J. (2017, October 24). Two States, a third of counties have more deaths than births. *The U.S. Census Bureau.* Retrieved from https://www.census.gov/library/stories/2017/10/aging-boomers-deaths.html

Duffin, E. (2020a, January 2). Marriage rate in the United States from 1990 to 2017 (per 1,000 of population). *Statistica.* Retrieved from https://www.statista.com/statistics/195951/marriage-rate-in-the-united-states-since-1990/

Duffin, E. (2020b, January 13). Average number of own children per U.S. family with own children 10960-2019. *Statistica.* Retrieved from https://www.statista.com/statistics/718084/average-number-of-own-children-per-family/

Frey, W. H. (2018, December 21). US Population growth hits 80-year low, capping off a year of demographic stagnation. *The Brookings Institute*. Retrieved from https://www.brookings.edu/blog/the-avenue/2018/12/21/us-population-growth-hits-80-year-low-capping-off-a-year-of-demographic-stagnation/##targetText=The%20just%2Dreleased%20census%20estimates,19.2%20million%20(8%20percent).

Hedegaard, H., Curtin, S., & Warner, M. (2018, June 18). Suicide rates in the United States continue to increase (NCHS Data Brief, no. 309). *Centers for Disease Control and Prevention*. Retrieved from https://www.cdc.gov/nchs/products/databriefs/db309.htm

Kochanek, K. D., Anderson, R. N., & Arias, E. (2020, January). Changes in life expectancy at birth, 2010–2018. *National Center for Health Statistics*. Retrieved from https://www.cdc.gov/nchs/data/hestat/life-expectancy/lifeexpectancy-H.pdf

Kochanek, K. D., Murphy, S. L., Xu, J., & Arias, E. (2017, December). Mortality in the United States, 2016 (NCHS Brief, no. 293). *Centers for Disease Control and Prevention*. Retrieved from https://www.cdc.gov/nchs/data/databriefs/db293.pdf

LaTour, A. (n.d.). Top 4 benefits of higher education. *Good Choices Good Life*. Retrieved from http://www.goodchoicesgoodlife.org/choices-for-young-people/the-benefits-of-higher-education/

Lopez, G., Ruiz, N., & Patten, E. (2017, September 8). Key facts about Asian Americans, a diverse and growing population. *The Pew Research Center*. Retrieved from https://www.pewresearch.org/fact-tank/2017/09/08/key-facts-about-asian-americans/

McMahon, T. (2020, April 3). What is the labor force participation rate? *UnemploymentData.com*. Retrieved from https://unemploymentdata.com/labor-force-participation-rate-2/

Murphy, S. L., Xu, J. Q., Kochanek, K. D., Arias, E. (2018, November). *Mortality in the United States, 2017* (NCHS Data Brief, no. 328). Center for Disease Control and Prevention. Retrieved from https://www.cdc.gov/nchs/data/databriefs/db328-h.pdf

National Oceanic and Atmospheric Administration. (2019, February 6). *National Climate Report*. Retrieved from https://www.ncdc.noaa.gov/sotc/national/201813

National Vital Statistics System. (2019). *10 Leading Causes of Death by Age Group United States–2018*. Retrieved from https://www.cdc.gov/injury/wisqars/pdf/leading_causes_of_death_by_age_group_2017-508.pdf

Northouse, P. G. (2019). *Leadership: Theory and practice (8th ed.)*. Sage.

Park, J. J. (2019, August 21). An uneven playing field: The complex educational experiences of Asian Americans. *Higher Education Today.* Retrieved from https://www.higheredtoday.org/2019/08/21/uneven-playing-field-complex-educational-experiences-asian-americans/

Saiidi, U. (2019, July 9). US life expectancy has been declining. Here's why. *Health and Science.* Retrieved from https://www.cnbc.com/2019/07/09/us-life-expectancy-has-been-declining-heres-why.html

Samenow, J. (2019, March 6). The United just had its wettest winter on record. *The Washington Post.* Retrieved from https://www.washingtonpost.com/weather/2019/03/06/united-states-just-witnessed-its-wettest-winter-recorded-history/

Schiller, B. R., & Gebhardt, K. (2017). *Essentials of economics* (10th ed.). New York: McGraw Hill.

Scholl, L., Seth, P., Mbabazi, K., Wilson, N., & Baldwin, G. (2019, January 4). Drug and opioid-involved overdose deaths—United States, 2013-2017. *Centers for Disease Control and Prevention.* Retrieved from https://www.cdc.gov/mmwr/volumes/67/wr/mm675152e1.htm?s_cid=mm675152e1_w

Solly, M. (2018, December 3). U.S. life expectancy drops for a third year in a row, reflecting rising drug overdoses, suicides. *Smithsonian.* Retrieved from https://www.smithsonianmag.com/smart-news/us-life-expectancy-drops-third-year-row-reflecting-rising-drug-overdose-suicide-rates-180970942/

Toossi, M. (2015, December). Labor force projections to 2024: The force is growing, but slowly. *Monthly Labor Review, U.S. Bureau of Labor Statistics.* Retrieved from https://www.bls.gov/opub/mlr/2015/article/labor-force-projections-to-2024.htm

Tran, V. C., Lee, J., & Huang, T. J. (2019). Revisiting the Asian second-generation advantage. *Ethnic and Racial Studies, 42*(13), 2248–2269.

U.S. Bureau of Labor Statistics. (2020a, January 10). *The employment situation—December 2019.* Retrieved from https://www.bls.gov/news.release/pdf/empsit.pdf

U.S. Bureau of Labor Statistics. (2020b, April 3). *The employment situation—March 2020.* Retrieved from https://www.bls.gov/news.release/pdf/empsit.pdf?mod=article_inline

U.S. Bureau of Labor Statistics. (2020c, May 8). *The employment situation—March 2020.* Retrieved from https://www.bls.gov/news.release/pdf/empsit.pdf?mod=article_inline

United States Census Bureau (USCB). (2018a, December). *Monthly population estimates for the United States: April 1, 2010 to December 1, 2019.* Retrieved from https://factfinder.census.gov/faces/tableservices/jsf/pages/productview.xhtml?src=bkmk#

United States Census Bureau (USCB). (2018b, September 18). *Projected population size and births, deaths, and migration: Main projections for the United States, 2017 to 2060.* Retrieved from https://www.census.gov/data/tables/2017/demo/popproj/2017-summary-tables.html

United States Census Bureau (USCB). (2019a, July 1). *Quick facts: Population estimates.* Retrieved from https://www.census.gov/quickfacts/fact/table/US/PST045219

United States Census Bureau (USCB). (2019b, February 21). *Educational attainment in the United States: 2018.* Retrieved from https://www.census.gov/data/tables/2018/demo/education-attainment/cps-detailed-tables.html

Walton, G. M., & Cohen, G. L. (2003). Stereotype lift. *Journal of Experimental Social Psychology, 39*(5), 456–467.

Wang, T. (2020, March 9). Average annual temperature in the U.S. from 1895 to 2018 (in Fahrenheit). *Statista.* Retrieved from https://www.statista.com/statistics/500472/annual-average-temperature-in-the-us/

WorldAtlas. (2016, July 7). *Geography Statistics of United States of America.* Retrieved from https://www.worldatlas.com/webimage/countrys/namerica/usstates/uslandst.htm

World Health Organization. (2018, April 6). *Life expectancy and healthy life expectancy.* Retrieved from http://apps.who.int/gho/data/view.main.SDG2016LEXREGv?lang=en

World Population Review. (2019). *Total Population by Country 2019.* Retrieved from http://worldpopulationreview.com/countries/

World Population Review. (2020). *The 200 Largest Cities in the United States by Population 2020.* Retrieved from http://worldpopulationreview.com/us-cities/

Xu, J. Q., Murphy, S. L., Kochanek, K. D., & Arias, E. (2020, January). Mortality in the United States, 2018 (NCHS Data Brief, no. 355). *Centers for Disease Control and Prevention.* Retrieved from https://www.cdc.gov/nchs/data/databriefs/db355-h.pdf

Zagorsky, J. L. (2016, June 1). Why are fewer people getting married? *The Conversation.* Retrieved from https://theconversation.com/why-are-fewer-people-getting-married-60301

Chapter 3

Technology and Innovation: Artificial Intelligence, Autonomous Vehicles, Drone Technology, and the Four Realities

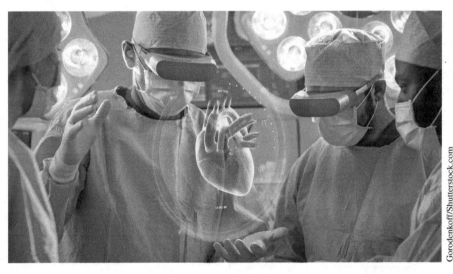

Gorodenkoff/Shutterstock.com

Technology and innovation continue to increase the speed at which we navigate our professional and personal lives and fuel unprecedented change along the way. Take the telephone, for example. The majority of the 20th century (1901–2000) used two simple phone models: the pulse-dialing rotary phone and the traditional touch-tone model, providing users with the basics to make and receive calls. In the last quarter of that century, cordless phones became

> **Technology:** Making, modification, usage, and knowledge of tools, machines, techniques, crafts, systems, and methods of organization.

both popular and affordable, and advancements in cellular technology and fiber optic cables paved the way for the introduction of new mobile device options for retail consumers (Goodwin, 2017). Now let's compare that to Apple, who has single-handedly introduced well over 50 models and variations of the iPhone and 20 versions of the iPad within their first 13 years of production. The multinational technology giant has now positioned itself as the leader in the smartwatch business, introducing five versions of the Apple Watch in as many years, and producing sales revenue that has elevated the business segment to the size of a Fortune 300 company by itself (Phelan, 2018).

Personal computers once designed on paper and assembled by hand are now designed on workstations and produced through a fully automated process.

> **Moore's Law:** The perception that the number of transistors on a microchip doubles every two years while the cost of computers declines resulting in increased speed and capabilities at lower costs. Moore's law posits exponential growth.

Computer chip capabilities continue to double regularly increasing speed as costs inversely continue to decline—a phenomenon known as **Moore's law**. Advancements in nanoengineering continue to facilitate the shift in energy from centralized nuclear power plants and liquid natural gas tankers to decentralized endpoints via solar energy (Kurzweil, 2019). As environmental sustainability continues to be a priority and lightweight fuel cells become more affordable, this form of technology will continue to experience exponential growth.

This megatrend continues to gain momentum as American industries (and consumers) become more dependent on technology and innovation to identify gaps, solve problems, improve situations, and address the increasing demand for new products and services.

> **Disruptor:** "Entrepreneurs, outsiders, and idealists (rather than industry insiders or market specialists) who create a product, service, or way of doing things which displaces the existing market leaders and eventually replaces them at the helm of the sector. Often linked to the fast-moving technology industry but can be found in almost any area of business. (Cotton, 2018)

Disruptors like Indigo Ag are using natural microbiology to improve sustainability and profits for growers, while Impossible Foods has produced a plant-based product that smells, cooks, and tastes like beef—the company has its sights set on eliminating the need for animals in the food system by 2035. Personal genetics company 23andMe now provides both ancestry information as well as genetic health risks and wellness measures (CNBC, 2019). These companies are following the path of pioneering "disruptor giants" like Uber, Amazon, and Netflix.

The SMAC (social, mobile, analytics, and cloud) movement and the increase of in-demand tech jobs such as AI architects, data scientists, developers, security professionals (data, information, network, and systems), and cloud administrators continue to direct traffic toward a variety of career paths in the tech sector. Futurists Bill Marr, Ray Kurzweil, and Thomas Frey, as well as thought-leading organizations like Accenture are all providing valuable insight into the role technology and innovation will play in the near future.

Artificial Intelligence

Artificial intelligence (AI) is defined as the branch of computer science dealing with the simulation of intelligent behavior in computers and the capability of a machine to imitate human behavior (Artificial Intelligence, n.d.; McCarthy, 2007). According to Sraders (2019), AI is the use of computer science programming to imitate human thought and action

> **Artificial Intelligence:** The branch of computer science dealing with the simulation of intelligent behavior in computers and the capability of a machine to imitate human behavior.

by analyzing data and surroundings, solving or anticipating problems, and learning or self-teaching to adapt to a variety of tasks. In simpler terms, Marr (2019a) describes AI as the idea of building machines with the "power to see, hear, taste, smell, touch, talk, walk, fly, and learn" like humans. Although definitions may vary slightly, the overarching concept of AI has remained consistent over its life span. AI is divided into three specialized areas: neural networks, **machine learning**, and deep learning.

> **Machine Learning:** Machine learning (ML) is the study of computer algorithms that improve automatically through experience.

Early on, AI platforms were mainly accessible to their proprietors (e.g., NVIDIA, Microsoft, Google). We now live in the fourth Industrial Revolution (Industry 4.0) where 5 of every 6 Americans are using AI and where AI tech leaders are contracting with universities and small start-ups, data scientists, and developers as an end-to-end service for building, testing, and deploying models. There has also been an emergence of a series of tier two level companies that have developed their own intelligent technology, offering customers the opportunity to utilize their AI platforms to produce algorithms and compute resources for a fee.

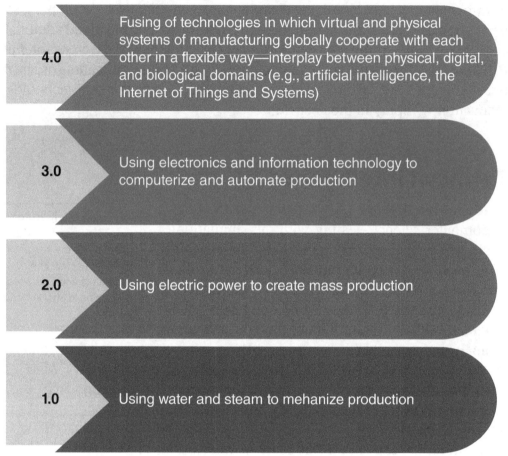

Schwab's Stages of Industrial Revolution

4.0 — Fusing of technologies in which virtual and physical systems of manufacturing globally cooperate with each other in a flexible way—interplay between physical, digital, and biological domains (e.g., artificial intelligence, the Internet of Things and Systems)

3.0 — Using electronics and information technology to computerize and automate production

2.0 — Using electric power to create mass production

1.0 — Using water and steam to mehanize production

Source: Schwab, 2016.

According to Roe (2018), AI is disrupting numerous industries, redefining them by automating processes, and providing greater personalization to users. Industries like agriculture, energy and mining, manufacturing, and retail are all integrating AI. In the healthcare sector, the Food and Drug Administration (FDA) is creating greater oversight and has already approved AI apps for strokes, bone health, vision science, and diabetic retinopathy detection (DePaolis, 2018; Hayes, 2019). AI is being used to identify "high-risk patient groups, automate diagnostic tests, increase speed and accuracy of treatment, improve drug formulations, and DNA analysis that can positively impact the quality of healthcare and affect human lives" (Roe, 2018, p. 1). AI is used in microscopy inside devices that bridge biology,

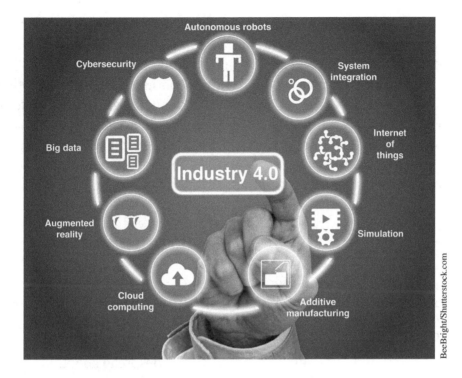

Autonomous robots

System integration

Cybersecurity

Internet of things

Big data

Industry 4.0

Augmented reality

Simulation

Cloud computing

Additive manufacturing

BeeBright/Shutterstock.com

optics, and nanotechnology. Computational modeling is already using algorithms so it is natural to expect that AI will play a significant role in nanocomputing and working with nanomaterials (Nano, 2018). Advancements in AI continue to lead us toward technological singularity, the hypothetical future point in time when ordinary human intelligence is overtaken by AI (Shanahan, 2015).

AI is what has made it possible for companies like Tesla, Toyota, and BMW to develop self-driving cars; and personal virtual assistants such as Siri, Alexa, Cortana, and Google Assistant to create reminders, take notes, set alarms, FaceTime people, make appointments, read notifications, and perform calculations (Klein, 2017; Tillman & Grabham, 2019). As biometric recognition moves toward becoming the norm, so does smart home control. Synching your mobile device with your home's security system, garage door, coffee machine, car, and wearable technology is appeasing the demand of a culture's growing dependency on convenience. Companies like Netflix and Spotify leverage AI and its predictive technology to recommend shows or artists based on viewing and listening preferences. Chatbots—computer programs designed to simulate conversation with human users and conversational agents—are replicating the patterns of human interactions and working somewhat independently. Companies like LivePerson power conversational commerce to increase sales and reduce costs. Advancements in machine learning are making customer support Live Chat services sound almost human and these entities continue to work toward eliminating the occasional awkward speech and cadence challenges. Retailers like Sephora, Dominos, Starbucks, and Staples as well as Fandango, the Wall Street Journal, and Mastercard all have successfully implemented chatbot campaigns. While writing this book, my life experience includes chatbot conversations with financial institutions, healthcare providers, and ride-hailing companies.

Autonomous Vehicles

Autonomous Vehicle Technology: The capability of driving a vehicle without the active physical control or monitoring by a human operator.

Autonomous vehicle (AV) technology is the capability of driving a vehicle without the active physical control or monitoring by a human operator. This technology has made significant progress over the past few years; however, we are not yet at a point where self-driving vehicles are ready for widespread adoption—there is still plenty of work to do before reaching level 5 automation. Nonetheless, it's one of the trends at the top of the list of enthused futurists and technologists.

Levels of Driving Automation

0	1	2	3	4	5
NO AUTOMATION	**DRIVER ASSISTANCE**	**PARTIAL AUTOMATION**	**CONDITIONAL AUTOMATION**	**HIGH AUTOMATION**	**FULL AUTOMATION**
Manual control. The human performs all driving tasks (steering, acceleration, braking, etc.)	The vehicle features a single automated system (e.g., it monitors speed through cruise control).	ADAS. The vehicle can perform steering and acceleration. The human still monitors all tasks and can take control at any time.	Environmental detection capabilities. The vehicle can perform most driving tasks, but human override is still required.	The vehicle performs all driving tasks under specific circumstances. Geofencing is required. Human override is still an option.	The vehicle performs all driving tasks under all conditions. Zero human attention or interaction is required.
THE HUMAN MONITORS THE DRIVING ENVIRONMENT			THE AUTOMATED SYSTEM MONITORS THE DRIVING ENVIRONMENT		

Source: Synopsys.com (2020). ©Kendall Hunt Publishing Company. Reprinted with permission.

According to the Coalition for Future Mobility (2020), AVs promise six potential benefits:

- Greater road safety: Reducing risky and dangerous driver behavior
- Greater independence: Increasing ride-sharing options promotes self-sufficiency for travelers including seniors and people with disabilities
- Cost-savings: Less financial resources spent on vehicle repairs, medical bills, lost time at work, and parking fees
- Increased productivity: Passengers can make calls, return emails, or watch a movie while in transit
- Reduced congestion: Less vehicles on the road equates to fewer "stop-and-go" waves and accidents
- Environmental gains: Less fuel reduces greenhouse gases, which in turn enhances the economic appeal and demand for electric vehicles

metamorworks/Shutterstock.com

Machine learning and the **Internet of Things (IoT)** technology have already begun enabling cars to teach themselves to drive by drawing on the rich data from the real world—the more they drive, the more data they collect on surroundings and traffic conditions. Waymo, Google's spinoff, is a pioneer in the field and is perhaps the recognized leader as they have been

Internet of Things (IoT): Everyday physical objects connected to the Internet, identifying themselves to other devices, acting in unison through ambient intelligence (Techopedia, 2019).

dabbling in the art and science of autonomous driving since 2009. The ride-hailing organization successfully piloted robotaxis in California and currently operates their Waymo One self-driving taxi in a 100-square-mile area serving four of Arizona's conservative Gridiron communities (Chandler, Gilbert, Mesa, & Tempe).

Many of the AV manufacturers have successfully completed tests; however, they continue to operate with humans in the vehicle for error. I agree with Bayern (2019) who posits that we are more likely to experience slower-moving shuttles and semipublic transportation operating in cities and dense urban areas on protected or semifixed routes before the launch of level 6, fully automated self-driving vehicles. Marr (2019b) highlights the notion that the industry has also benefited from other in-car advancements that have occurred in tandem while working with autonomous driving technology such as security and entertainment functions—all of which have increased reliance on data capture and analytics.

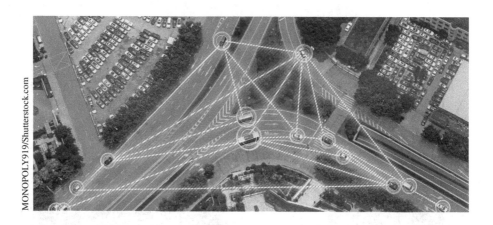

MONOPOLY919/Shutterstock.com

Drone Technology

The earliest records of unmanned aerial vehicles (UAVs) dates back to 1849 when the Austrians attacked the Italian city of Venice using unmanned balloons loaded with explosives. Drone technology has since come a long way and UAVs now operate as a component of the unmanned aircraft system, which consists of a ground-based controller and a system that facilitates communication between the two. Although the early application was military-focused, drones today operate in agriculture, emergency medical services, entertainment, construction, and thermal imaging. Drones vary in size—some are as large as small aircraft and transport cargo while others like the DARPA Nano Hummingbird measure 6.5 inches) and are used in surveillance. Hammacher Schlemmer produces a 1.1-inch square quadcopter that can be launched from the tip of a thumb.

Bloomberg/Bloomberg/Getty Images

Drone technology is used in real estate to facilitate land surveying and mapping, produce promotional pictures and videos, and capture the data needed to import into CAD (computer-aided design) systems for design and simulation in real-world conditions. Architects, engineers, and inspectors now have an additional cost-effective resource to leverage when developing properties through **photogrammetry** and troubleshooting logistical challenges and construction barriers. Ag-specific drones are being used to help optimize agricultural operations by creating prescription maps to manage farms and assisting with crop health. One-third of all rice consumed in Japanese homes is produced using

> **Photogrammetry:**
> The science of making measurements through the use of photographs, especially aerial photographs.

drones (Francis, 2017)—drones provide high-tech support for aging rice farmers and to a country that is experiencing a shortage in the next generation of farmers (Obayashi, 2018). Drones identify irrigation issues, soil variances, and pest and fungal infestations. Multispectral imaging shows both a visual spectrum and a near-infrared view assisting farmers in differentiating between healthy and unhealthy crops. Drones fly in varying conditions, provide a data-rich alternative to scouting crops, and can proactively be utilized to improve crop health by spraying pesticides. Commercial drone tech company PrecisionHawk's motto says it all: "Don't walk the field—fly it."

For the 2018 Winter Olympics in Pyeongchang, Intel designed a digital fireworks show using a swarm of 1,218 synchronized drones (a world record) to create an animated air dance of a three-dimensional figure.

Marco Caduff/EyeEm via Getty Images

Thousands of drones were used to put on a pre-recorded light show during the opening ceremony for the 2018 Winter Olympics in Pyeongchang, South Korea, on Feb. 9, 2018.

Disney uses the same technology to enhance performance by creating flying displays, projection screens, projectors, and as puppeteers for flying puppet shows. They even have airbag drones that deploy on detecting a condition warranting activation (Patent Yogi, n.d.). NASA, the National Aeronautics and Space Administration, has scheduled its Mars 2020 launch for the third quarter of 2020 and has attached a Mars drone helicopter to the rover's belly in preparation for exploration when it lands in February 2021. The twin-rotor, solar-powered drone will be the first aircraft to fly on another planet (NASA, 2019).

Medical drones are being used to traverse mountainous terrain and deliver shipments of medication to pop-up clinics (Graboyas & Bryan, 2019). They have the ability to operate in varying weather conditions to quickly deliver blood, vaccines, and various medical supplies. Netherland-based TU Delft has designed ambulance drones that can prevent death and speed up recovery times. They have integrated lifesaving technology such as Automated External Defibrillators (AED), medication, and Cardiopulmonary Resuscitation (CPR) aids compact enough to be carried by a drone (TUDelft, 2020).

Ambulance Drone

Today's drones can fly autonomously utilizing state-of-the-art AI technology in conjunction with flight plans embedded in their systems, onboard sensors, and GPS. **Edge computing** is bringing computational infrastructure, data storage, and automation to the location where it is needed, saving bandwidth and improving response times. Instead of relying on the cloud at a centralized data center to do all the work, the cloud is coming to the "edge of the action," performing on decentralized distributed devise nodes, reducing the flow of data traffic providing real-time local data analysis (SPEC India, 2019).

Edge Computing:
A decentralized and distributed computing paradigm that's operates at or near the data source.

Drones are also flying about delivering packages, performing utility work, conducting structural inspections, and route mapping. They are used in facial recognition and archaeology alike and pilots are using these aerial assets to estimate beehive populations as well as to film the latest Hollywood blockbuster. As long as the challenges with low-altitude airspace operations are addressed and managed, drone technology will continue to flourish.

The Four Realities

According to Marr (2019a), AI will continue to enhance the use of augmented reality (AR) and virtual reality (VR) technologies as algorithms become more sophisticated and improve computer vision—a function that allows computers to understand what they see through cameras. Siglin (2018) and Fourtané (2018) have observed that this technology is also experiencing applications in mediums called mixed reality (MR) and extended reality (XR). **Augmented reality (AR)** is a technology that superimposes a computer-generated image on a user's view of the real world—a composite view if you will. The Pokémon Company uses an AR functionality with its Pokémon GO game that challenges its 67 million users to explore, discover, and collect creatures across the planet.

> **Augmented Reality (AR):** A technology that superimposes a computer-generated image on a user's view of the real world.

Wachiwit/Shutterstock.com

The Sky Guide app uses the GPS features on the iPhone or iPad smart device to deliver star maps that reflect the way the sky looks above at the precise moment and the Measure app allows users to take rough measurements of objects using the device's camera (Johnson, 2019). AR has made its way into manufacturing, automotive repair, and orthopedic and trauma surgery.

Virtual reality (VR) is the digital recreation of a real-life setting that puts users inside of a three-dimensional interactive computer-generated environment by using special electronic equipment such as a helmet with special lenses or gloves fitted with sensors. This creates a 360-degree digital experience that can be similar or completely different from a real-world experience. Becker (2020) predicts that the installed base of VR headsets are estimated to reach 82 million units worldwide by 2020 and that numerous industries will continue adopting the technology. People will be able to be virtually transported to other parts of the world and to areas that exist only in their imagination. An individual with limited traveling capabilities and diving skills might explore a shipwreck deep in the Bermuda Triangle or visit the Arashiyama Bamboo Grove in Japan. Lowe's Innovation Labs and Microsoft have tested VR technology in its

> **Virtual Reality (VR):**
> The digital re-creation of a real-life setting that puts users inside of a three-dimensional interactive computer-generated environment by using special electronic equipment such as a helmet with special lenses or gloves fitted with sensors.

alphaspirit/Shutterstock.com

"Holoroom How to" space where consumers can learn basic do-it-yourself (DIY) skills in a fun interactive environment. Consumers can learn how to paint a fence, tile a shower, and previsualize numerous appliance and cabinet combinations for their homes. In the film and television industry, VR users will be able to experience movies as a character in the story.

MR combines elements of both real and virtual environments creating a new world where physical and synthetic elements interact together (Shaptunova, 2018). Consider a digital overlay on a car windshield, for example.

metamorworks/Shutterstock.com

Luxury car manufacturer BMW unveiled its BMW I Interactive Ease windshield which uses a contextual user interface, intelligent lighting, and adaptable interior that looks more like a hotel suite than a passenger vehicle. As you travel, you can leverage the Intelligent Personal Assistant and overlay information about points of interest within the passenger's field of view, convert the cabin to a mobile theater (compete with ambient lighting), turn seats into an interactive surface, and recline to emulate a sense of weightlessness (Palladino, 2020). In the global marketplace, this hybrid reality technology will give meeting participants a feeling as if they were in the same room with other team colleagues, even if they are halfway across the globe. Spatial Systems, Inc. (spatial.io) is a collective computing platform that allows individuals to connect through a shared spatial audio and three-dimensional telepresence, unlocking the team's productive and creative potential. Although the technology is not quite at the level of producing holographic meetings that mimic a Star Wars Jedi Council gathering, the technology is developing so rapidly that it may become the baseline standard in the next 3 to 5 years.

Golden Sikorka/Shutterstock.com

Finally, **extended reality (XR)** refers to the blended and combined use of real environments, virtual environments, and human—machine interactions generated by computer technology and wearables. In essence, XR encompasses the entire spectrum of the reality—virtuality continuum (VR, AR, and MR), including all future realities that this technology may bring. Marr (2019c) refers to the construct as an "umbrella term for all the immersive technologies that merge the physical and virtual worlds." Scribani (2019) describes how this disruption will facilitate our future workday at the office:

> **Extended Reality (XR):**
> The blending and combining use of real environments, virtual environments, and human-machine interactions generated by computer technology and wearables.

It's the year 2030, and you have a busy day scheduled. You need to check on your production lines in China, visit Mars on your lunch break, and attend a business meeting in Brazil—all from the comfort of your New York office.

Although early in its life cycle, extended reality is currently being leveraged in high-risk military training operations as well as in the medical, manufacturing, and marketing industries. Educators and training delivery specialists are also utilizing XR to develop cost-effective, immersive learning experiences that imitate a professional workplace setting. Event planners, real estate agents, and retailers are among the many professionals moving toward improving the customer experience through XR. I would be remiss however if I did not issue a proper caution—it is equally important to understand that as this technology becomes seamless and routine, the threat of cyberattack increases exponentially. Without proper cybersecurity hygiene and threat intelligence, organizations will experience unprecedented levels of supply chain attacks, data breaches, and threats to the cloud ecosystem.

Sergey Nivens/Shutterstock.com

Discussion Questions

1. Identify three specific instances of AI that currently influence the way you live and work, etc. Among them, identify at least one negative AI experience and discuss its undesirable impact.

2. Identify and discuss a specific industry that has been disrupted by AI. What role has AI played in the industry. How did the industry benefit from AI? What problem did AI solve? What gap did AI fill?

3. Conduct some research and discuss the barriers that are getting in the way of reaching level 5 driving automation? Discuss three advantages and disadvantages of self-driving vehicles.

4. Conduct some research on drone technology. Identify three specific uses of drone technology that have not been discussed. Describe three advantages and disadvantages of drone technology and application.

5. Define virtual reality (VR), augmented reality (AR), mixed reality (MR), and extended reality (XR) with one concise sentence each. Then discuss a specific example of reality.

References

Artificial Intelligence. (n.d.). In *Merriam-Webster's collegiate dictionary.* Retrieved January 29, 2020, from https://www.merriam-webster.com/dictionary/artificial%20intelligence

Bayern, M. (2019, November 4). The top 3 companies in autonomous vehicles and self-driving cars. *Zdnet.com.* Retrieved from https://www.zdnet.com/article/the-top-3-companies-in-autonomous-vehicles-and-self-driving-cars/

Becker, B. (2020). 9 VR marketing examples that you will want to steal for 2020. *Hubspot.* Retrieved from https://blog.hubspot.com/marketing/vr-marketing-examples

CNBC. (2019, May 15). *Meet the 2019 NBC disruptor 50 companies.* Retrieved from https://www.cnbc.com/2019/05/14/23andme-2019-disruptor-50.html

Coalition for Future Mobility. (2020). *Benefit of self-driving vehicles.* Retrieved from https://coalitionforfuturemobility.com/benefits-of-self-driving-vehicles/

Cotton, B. (2018, September 27). What is a disruptor? *Business Leader.* Retrieved from https://www.businessleader.co.uk/what-is-a-disruptor/52464/

DePaolis, M. D. (2018). It is our job to harness AI in medicine. *Primary Care Optometry News, 23*(8), 3.

Fourtané, S. (2018). 5 technology trends to watch in 2019. *Interesting Engineering.* Retrieved from https://interestingengineering.com/5-technology-trends-to-watch-in-2019

Francis, R. (2017). 10 unusual uses for drones. *B & H Photo Video.* Retrieved from https://www.bhphotovideo.com/explora/video/tips-and-solutions/10-unusual-uses-drones?BI=572&gclid=EAIaIQobChMItpGC14Ct5wIVsRx9C h2ArQUBEAAYASAAEgJOw_D_BwE

Goodwin, R. (2017, May 6). The history of mobile phones from 1973 to 2008: The handsets that made it all happen. *Know Your Mobile.* Retrieved from https://www.knowyourmobile.com/nokia/nokia-3310/19848/history-mobile-phones-1973-2008-handsets-made-it-all-happen

Graboyas, R., & Bryan, D. N. (2019, January 18). Drones delivering medical supplies and more can help save American lives. *Statnews.* Retrieved from https://www.statnews.com/2019/01/18/drones-deliver-medical-supplies-united-states/

Hayes, T. (2019). The FDA is making rules for AI in medicine. *Healthcare Packaging.* Retrieved from http://eres.regent.edu:2048/login?url=https://search-proquest-com.ezproxy.regent.edu/docview/2209701436?accountid=13479

Johnson, L. (2019, April 22). 10 augmented reality apps for iPhone and iPad you should be using right now. *Macworld.* Retrieved from https://www.macworld.com/article/3390180/best-augmented-reality-ar-apps-for-ios-iphone-ipad.html

Klein, M. (2017, July 10). 26 actual useful things that you could do with Siri. *How-to Geek.* Retrieved from https://www.howtogeek.com/229308/26-actually-useful-things-you-can-do-with-siri/

Kurzweil, R. [TED Conferences] (2019, November 17). *The accelerated power of technology* [Video]. Retrieved from https://www.ted.com/talks/ray_kurzweil_the_accelerating_power_of_technology?language=en#t-151013

Marr, B. (2019a). *Artificial intelligence in practice: How 50 successful companies used AI and machine learning to solve problems.* John Wiley & Sons, Ltd.

Marr, B. (2019b, January 14). 5 important augmented and virtual reality trends for 2019 everyone should read. *Forbes.* Retrieved from https://www.forbes.com/sites/bernardmarr/2019/01/14/5-important-augmented-and-virtual-reality-trends-for-2019-everyone-should-read/#53ac2eab22e7

Marr, B. (2019c, August 12). What is extended reality technology? A simple explanation for everyone. *Forbes.* Retrieved from https://www.forbes.com/sites/bernardmarr/2019/08/12/what-is-extended-reality-technology-a-simple-explanation-for-anyone/#4bbe5ec97249

McCarthy, J. (2007). *What is artificial intelligence?* Stanford University Press.

Nano. (2018, August 22). The convergence of AI and nanotechnology. Retrieved from https://nano-magazine.com/news/2018/8/22/the-convergence-of-ai-and-nanotechnology

NASA. (2019, August 27). NASA Mars helicopter attached to Mars 2020 rover. Retrieved from https://www.nasa.gov/feature/jpl/nasas-mars-helicopter-attached-to-mars-2020-rover

Obayashi, Y. (2018, August 23). Drones offer high-tech help to Japan's aging farmers. *Reuters.* Retrieved from https://www.reuters.com/article/us-japan-farming-drones/drones-offer-high-tech-help-to-japans-aging-farmers-idUSKCN1L80TX

Palladino, T. (2020, January 9). BMW augmented reality windshield concept adds gaze detection for natural interaction. *Next Reality News.* Retrieved from https://next.reality.news/news/bmw-augmented-reality-windshield-concept-adds-gaze-detection-for-natural-interaction-0228950/

Patent Yogi. (n.d.). *Disney invents crazy drone technology.* Retrieved from https://patentyogi.com/latest-patents/disney/disney-invented-airbags-drones/

Phelan, D. (2018, Feb 15). Apple CEO reveals watch business approaching Fortune 300-size company. *Forbes.* Retrieved from https://www.forbes.com/sites/davidphelan/2018/02/15/apple-ceo-reveals-watch-business-approaching-fortune-300-size-company/#5e37b4872217

Roe, D. (2018, April 27). 11 industries being disrupted by AI. *CMSWIRE.* Retrieved from https://www.cmswire.com/information-management/11-industries-being-disrupted-by-ai/

Scribani, J. (2019, January 16). What is extended reality (XR)? *Visual Capitalist.* Retrieved from https://www.visualcapitalist.com/extended-reality-xr/

Shanahan, M. (2015). *The technological singularity.* Cambridge, MA: The MIT Press.

Shaptunova, Y. (2018, August 24). What is extended reality and what can we do with it? *SaM Solutions.* Retrieved from https://www.sam-solutions.com/blog/what-is-extended-reality-and-what-can-we-do-with-it/

Siglin, T. (2018, June 13). AR, MR, XR, VR streaming: Understanding the 4R's. *Wowza Media Systems.* Retrieved from https://www.wowza.com/blog/ar-mr-xr-and-vr-streaming-understanding-the-4-rs

Spec India. (2019, June 24). What is edge computing? The quick overview explained with examples. *Codeburst.* Retrieved from https://codeburst.io/what-is-edge-computing-the-quick-overview-explained-with-examples-bc8e1ec5b9a0

Sraders, A. (2019, January 3). What is artificial intelligence? Examples and news in 2019. *TheStreet.* Retrieved from https://www.thestreet.com/technology/what-is-artificial-intelligence-14822076

Synopsys. (2020). *Dude, where is my autonomous car? The 6 levels of vehicle autonomy.* Retrieved from https://www.synopsys.com/automotive/autonomous-driving-levels.html

Tillman, M., & Grabham, D. (2019, January 9). What is Google Assistant and what can it do? *Pocket-lint.* Retrieved from https://www.pocket-lint.com/apps/news/google/137722-what-is-google-assistant-how-does-it-work-and-which-devices-offer-it

TUDelft. (2020). *Ambulance Drone.* Retrieved from https://www.tudelft.nl/en/ide/research/research-labs/applied-labs/ambulance-drone/

Chapter 4

Technology and Innovation: Automation, Robotics, 3D Printing, Mobile EcoSystem, and Gamification

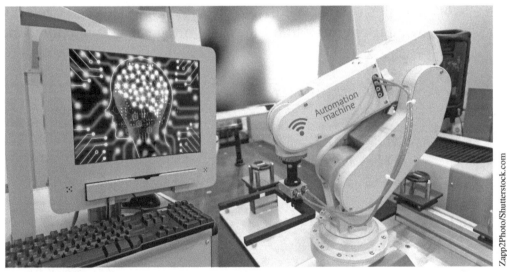

Zapp2Photo/Shutterstock.com

I recently had the opportunity to have two inspiring interactions relating to technology that I would like to share as we continue our journey exploring the megatrend of technology and innovation. Rob Ryan founded and sold his Internet company, Ascend Communications, to Lucent Technologies for $24 billion in 1999. Rob taught me a valuable lesson: the essence of being a great

Innovation: A new idea, method, or device; the introduction of something new.

entrepreneur is having an innovative mindset. **Innovation** is the foundation of the entrepreneurial spirit, and it drives us to identify gaps, solve problems, and improve current methods. Innovation is the driving force that inspires the technology megatrend which has catapulted the United States into becoming one of the world's most technologically advanced countries (Getzoff, 2020).

Dr. Rick Martinez introduced me to the concept of Age of Acceleration, which considers the relationship between the rates of technological innovation and human adaptability. As we continue transitioning deeper into the era of artificial intelligence, Dr. Martinez posits that the rate of innovation is moving at a pace that has already exceeded that of the human ability to adapt (see Figure 4.1), creating more technopeasantry along the way. The gradual elastic incline representing the rate of human adaptability is no match for the monstrous rise in the rate of technological innovation (Martinez, 2019). As a result, we are now at that point where the only way to lift the slope of human adaptability to meet the

FIGURE 4.1 The Age of Acceleration

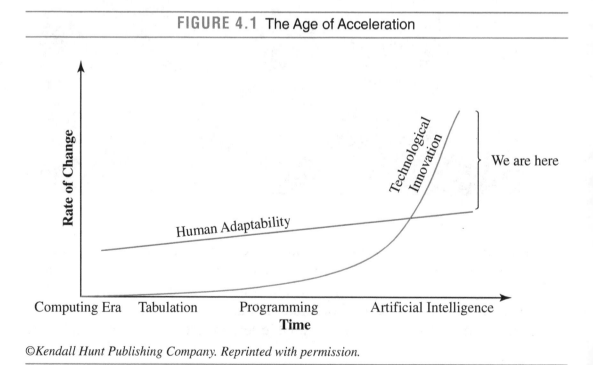

demands of technological innovation is to increase the speed of learning through governance and education (Friedman, 2017).

In the previous chapter, we considered the impact that artificial intelligence, automated driving, drone technology, and the four realities have on shaping our perspectives of the world in which we live. In this chapter, we continue our exploration into the technology and innovation megatrend by surveying automation in its various forms, including robotics and 3D scanning and printing, as well as discussing the mobile ecosystem and gamification.

Automation

Automation means using computer software, machines, or other technology to carry out tasks that would otherwise be done by human workers. Automation continues to gain momentum as machines, robots, and algorithms replace professional jobs traditionally done by humans in the fields of accounting, law, health care, and financial services (Gerber, 2019). Scripts run at the same time each day to clean up disk space on web servers, operating systems self-repair broken files, and front doors unlock as occupants approach with groceries. Interactive Bluetooth speakers provide voice assistants that can answer quick questions, manage appointments, and connect to third-party services such as restaurants and music streaming services. In the auto industry, laser diodes allow automobile manufacturers to create "invisible" welds on car shells that provide additional structural security while reducing car weight, production time, and energy costs (Arnold Machine, 2020).

The Recession of 2008 sparked a surge of innovative advancements in the retail banking sector. Digital payment services like PayPal, Amazon Pay, WePay, and Venmo were first movers into the e-commerce arena, facilitating payments between parties via online transfers connected to users' credit cards or checking accounts.

> **Automation:** Using computer software, machines, and other technology to carry out tasks that would otherwise be done by human workers (Owen-Hill, 2017).

> **Recession:** A significant decline in economic activity spread across the economy, lasting more than a few months, normally visible in real GDP, real income, employment, industrial production, and wholesale-retail sales (National Bureau of Economic Research, 2020).

> **First-Mover Advantage:** The advantage and benefit that comes to an organization because it exploits an opportunity before any other organization.

These digital payment platforms laid the framework for companies like Square to begin supporting small business transactions through readers and point-of-sale software. Google Wallet, Apple Pay, Google Pay, and Zelle have since followed, increasing digital payment capabilities in stores, in apps, and on the web. Improvements in the field have also allowed for a series of robust advancements such as contactless payment technology, large-volume processing, online and offline solutions, and protection through multiple layers of security. Internationally, Alibaba Group's third-party online payment platform Alipay processes more than half of China's transactions servicing 600 million registered users in a virtually cashless society (Technavio, 2019).

Along with advancements in electronic bill pay and instant photo check deposits, the functionality of Automatic Teller Machines (ATMs) has also increased significantly in the wake of the economic downturn of 2008. As retail banks explored new avenues to elevate the customer experience and manage costs, ATM performance improved dramatically, leading to the development of what banks today call Intelligent Teller Machines (ITMs) or electronic Automatic Teller Machines (eATMs). Today's features include interactive touch screens, options to deposit both checks and cash simultaneously without an envelope, identification technology access without a physical ATM card (using a smart device), dispensing customized

cozyta/Shutterstock.com

denominations of currency, and the ability to make direct payments to customer credit cards. ATMs also provide targeted commercials, promotional offers, and personal notes such as birthday greetings and holiday messages. Financial institutions are now beginning to pilot this technology to send customized messages to your smart device as you enter their banking center.

Over the last decade, retail banking centers have reduced their FTE (full-time equivalent) and customers continue to enjoy the robust features from their ATMs. ATM technology has created efficiencies by increasing the length of time between cash replenishment cycles through cash recycling. Today, predictive maintenance practices (over traditional time-based preventive maintenance) help determine the

> **Full-Time Equivalent (FTE):** A measure that allows the company to calculate the equivalent number of full-time employees it would have in a given period of time.

condition of in-service equipment and assist in estimating when maintenance should be performed. I had the opportunity to discuss these challenges with Henry Walker, president of Farmers and Merchants Bank, a regional bank in Southern California with nearly $7 billion in assets under management. In a conversation regarding the importance of the customer experience in light of dependence on ATM technology, Walker highlighted the fact that ATM and mobile technologies are highly beneficial; however, they are limiting the "customer touchpoints and challenging banks to seek new ways to make a connection" (H. Walker, personal communication, May 15, 2019).

ATM technology has crossed over into other industries as well. McDonald's, Home Depot, and Walmart have all integrated checkout technology into their centers, facilitating both ordering and paying for items. Cardpool, a gift card exchange program, has kiosks in retailers like Vons and Target to provide consumers the opportunity to buy and sell gift cards at discounted prices (Cardpool, 2020). GOLD to go™ Vending Machines (aka Gold ATMs) allow consumers to purchase gold and jewelry at the push of a button from a machine that updates prices every minute. EcoATM™ uses the technology in its ATMs to evaluate and offer customers instant cash for their used device (smart device, cell phone, MP3 player, etc.) (ecoATM, 2019). Finally, there are a series of specialized ATM machines throughout California that provide the consumer with the option to purchase and sell Bitcoin currency

> **Bitcoin:** A decentralized digital currency (cryptocurrency) without a central bank or single administrator that can be sent from user to user on the peer-to-peer bitcoin network without the need for intermediaries.

(BitcoinPlug, 2020; RockitCoin, 2020). ATM technology is becoming more popular among consumers, new and old, and they are finding tremendous value in integrating this technology with the smart devices they now use on a regular basis—convenience is king.

Self-checkout registers area in a Target store in south San Francisco bay area

Human Resource Management: The design of formal systems in an organization to manage human talent for accomplishing organizational goals (Mathis et al., 2017, p. 5).

Human resource (HR) management departments are using automation and intelligent software solutions to proactively interact with all stages of the employee life cycle. Data collection and processes relating to recruiting, onboarding, performance evaluation and management, benefits administration, employee turnover, and exit interviewing can all be streamlined using one of many efficient human resources information systems (HRIS). Big data and employee analytics are being leveraged to comprehend and engage teams within organizations and reveal patterns and trends relating to human behavior. HR management systems also facilitate planning, communication, and forecasting, as well as provide the tactical data utilized in the mining of competitive intelligence. A growing number of industries combine artificial intelligence and automation; however, it is essential to note that AI and automation are two distinct genres (Morikawa, 2017). Nicastro (2018) suggested that these automated systems, in conjunction with AI, enhance the selection process and candidate experience by scheduling interviews, providing real-time feedback to candidates, and answering questions. They assist in automating low-value add tasks, minimizing language and unconscious biases, and providing valuable insight as to who is committed to the organization and who may be "fixing" to leave. Algorithms analyze employee computer activity (e.g., pattern and tone of communication, keystroke activity, Internet browsing time), providing quantitative data that indicates how employees may be feeling about their role, department, or place within the organization. Freeing up HR professionals from mundane (but still important) time-consuming tasks creates opportunities to make the trek toward the design and execution of larger-scale strategic initiatives addressing business realities, focusing on future requirements, and how the management of human capital aligns with organizational objectives (Mathis et al., 2017).

> **Competitive Intelligence:** Defining, gathering, analyzing, and distributing intelligence about competitors, and any aspect of the environment needed to support an organization in strategic decision making (e.g., products, services, etc.).

> **Human Capital:** The collective value of the capabilities, knowledge, skills, life experiences, and motivation of an organization's workforce (Mathis et al., 2017).

Alexander Supertramp/Shutterstock.com

Robotics

> **Robotics:** Using computer software, machines, and other technology to carry out tasks that would otherwise be done by human workers (Owen-Hill, 2017).

Robotics is the interdisciplinary and interfacing branch of engineering and computer science which incorporates multiple disciplines to design, build, program, and use robotic machines. It is an interactive environment where computer software, machines, and other technology carry out tasks that would otherwise be done by human workers (Owen-Hill, 2017). Robotics is changing the world by helping humankind do tasks with greater efficiency and effectiveness. Robots are employed to support warehouse logistics and in manufacturing assembly lines to assemble, weld, and paint; they also "machine tend" meaning that they can proactively inspect, wash, deburr, sort, pack, and gauge. Their menu of tasks goes beyond the traditional loading and unloading of materials. Amazon, for example, leverages a series of drive units, palletizers, and robo-stows in their fulfillment centers to help optimize the supply chain and improve the customer experience (Amazon, n.d.).

Chesky/Shutterstock.com

Robotics will also continue to increase its presence in exploration and navigation. Earlier, we discussed NASA's scheduled launch of its twin-rotor, solar-powered Mars drone helicopter as part of the technological megatrend. Robots will also lead the way in ocean exploration. Mining the deep seas of the Central and Eastern Manus Basin in the Pacific with cutting and collecting robots will provide access to valuable metals and treasures at depths too dangerous to operate otherwise. According to Morrison (2020), the U.S. Navy is developing the next generation of unmanned robot submarines (controlled by AI) that will have the capability to surveil for months before requiring any maintenance. These autonomous undersea weapon systems will protect shores and waters by advanced communication and possess weapon systems that could be used to diffuse mines and sink targets if necessary.

The environment is also benefiting from advancements in ocean exploration. Liquid Robotics, a strategic partnership between the National Oceanic and Atmospheric Administration (NOAA) and a Boeing subsidiary, has created a series of surface ocean robots with research capabilities that can gather data on the acidity, alkalinity (pH), and salinity levels from water samples (Herbert, 2017).

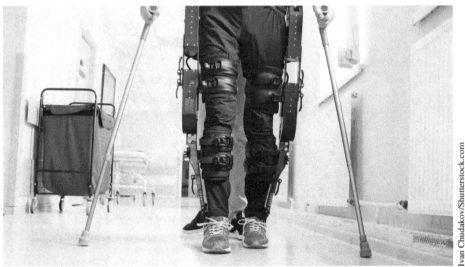

Ivan Chudakov/Shutterstock.com

In health care, robot exoskeletons have emerged as wearable units that restore locomotion. Controlled by computer boards powering a system of motors, pneumatics, levers, or hydraulics, powered exoskeletons serve as a "rehabilitation tool that may ameliorate several of the existing health-related consequences after spinal cord injury" (Gregory, 2018, p. 1). Once considered a unique sci-fi fashion accessory in movies like Aliens, The Avengers, and Avatar, exoskeletons currently offer a plethora of modern-day application—construction, firefighting and rescue work, military operations—in an effort at minimizing arm, back, neck, and shoulder injuries. Ford tasked Ekso Bionics to design an adjustable exoskeleton to reduce the risk of work-related medical issues. In 2018, the Ford Motor Company piloted, then debuted, the EksoVest in 15 automotive plants worldwide (Crowe, 2018).

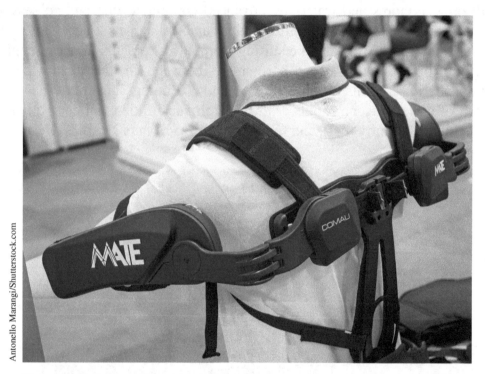

Antonello Marangi/Shutterstock.com

The exoskeletons like this one reduces workforce injuries caused by repetitive motion.

Hansen Robotics has combined AI and robotics to design and develop Sophia, an advanced human-crafted science fiction character depicting the future of AI and robotics (Hansen Robotics, n.d.). According to Hansen Robotics, Sophia is the world's first robot citizen and Innovation Ambassador for the United Nations Development Programme. Considered hybrid human AI, Sophia's unique

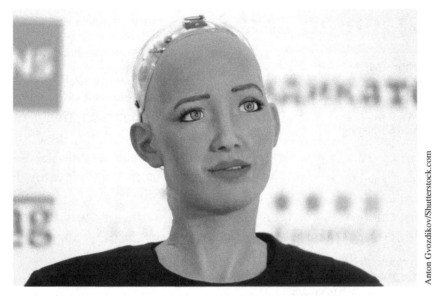

Hanson Robotics' most advanced human-like robot, Sophia.

combination of science, engineering, and artistry have all led to the humanizing of AI. Through conference and television appearances, Sophia continues to create awareness and promote a platform for advanced robotics and AI research.

The field of robotics continues to advance with several new technological achievements. **Big data** now offers more opportunity to build programming capability into robotic systems, and new developments in sensor technology allow connected devices to monitor environmental aspects like temperature, air pressure, light, and motion. In other areas of business and commerce, **robotic process automation (RPA)** has made its way into data migration, call center operations, application interpretation, as well as serving as information aggregators and metasearch engines. Growing careers in RPA include business analysis, solution architecture, consulting, and project management (Srivastava, 2017).

Big Data: Extremely large data sets that may be analyzed computationally to reveal patterns, trends, and associations, especially relating to human behavior and interactions.

Robotic Process Automation (RPA): The use of software to automate business processes to capture and interpret applications for processing transactions, manipulating data, triggering responses and communicating with other digital systems (Boulton, 2018).

3D Scanning and Printing

> **3D Printing:** The process of making a physical object from a three-dimensional digital model, typically by laying down many thin layers of a material in succession (additive manufacturing).

3D printing technology, also known as additive manufacturing, has made its way into industry. Today, the technology is leveraged across a broad range of industries including manufacturing, oil and gas, education, aerospace, agriculture, medicine, high tech, sports, and the three that make up the AEC—architecture, engineering, and construction (Javelin Technologies, 2019). The term "additive" refers to the successive addition of thin layers between 16 and 180 microns or more to create an object. 3D printing consists of three steps: preparation (CAD, 3D scanning, or downloaded file), actual printing, and finishing (Sculpteo, 2019).

I remember my first experience watching this advanced scanning technique "in action" around 2001 when the process was still developing. I was working on a film project in the entertainment industry and was invited to visit a leading 3D scanning facility just after they had completed a scan of an A-list celebrity. They used the digital data to create a 3D character model of the actor to produce an animated sequence, complete with digital visual effects. They also used the scan to produce a prosthetic mask that was used by a stunt double in a live-action sequence. The two scenes were edited together in the final cut and rolled flawlessly on the big screen.

New Story is a more current example of how this technology is being used. Inspired by an increasing level of homelessness in Haiti, 20-something's Brett Hagler, Alexandria Lafci, and Matthew Marshall cofounded New Story, a nonprofit focused on global homelessness, a problem that is projected to affect three billion people by 2050. New Story joined forces with construction technology company ICON and began revolutionizing the home building process using 3D printing technology to build homes for families in need. Each home can be built in 24 hours at a cost of $6,000. The strategic partnership between the two organizations is spearheading the building of the world's first 3D community (New Story, 2018, 2019).

In the medical industry, 3D printing is revolutionizing the methods in which health care is improving and saving lives. 3D printing facilitates medical training for future doctors by giving them realistic models that mimic human

A similar 3D housing printer along with finished walls of a 3D house.

parts and organs (Leapfrog, n.d.). Practicing on humanlike parts increases the quality of skills doctors obtain during training. New developments in 3D printing are transforming lives with better-fitting and better-looking prosthetics. Advances in 3D scanning technology are improving the design of customized sockets, speed of personalized prosthetic fittings and manufacturing, for a more comfortable and faster fit all while simultaneously driving costs down (The Garage, 2019). Typically, prosthetics need to be replaced every 3 to 5 years due to wear and tear, so low-cost production vehicles provide consumers with more options.

> **Developing Country:**
> A country with a less developed industrial base and a low Human Development Index (HDI) relative to other countries.

According to the World Health Organization (2005), there are over 30 million amputees around the world, four of every five who live in a **developing country**. 3D printing technology provides an affordable solution for those that live in developing countries. The BRICs (Brazil, Russia, India, and China) are considered the largest of the emerging markets moving toward reclassification. Other developing countries include newly industrialized countries such as Indonesia, Mexico, and the Philippines (Kuepper, 2019). In war-torn countries like Syria, Iraq, and Afghanistan, 3D printing technology is being sent in advance to print the additive manufacturing gear needed to produce the actual prosthetics, keeping resource and shipping costs down. As odd as it sounds, the printing equipment is actually "printing equipment and parts" to produce prosthetics. In the United States, companies like Naked Prosthetics and Will Root are working in consultation with clinics, independent prosthetists, physicians, and surgeons to provide prostheses that are simple and fully functional for everyday use. The 3D production process has become relatively streamlined—developments in scanning, modeling, and additive manufacturing have paved the way for the 3D production of customizable bionic eyes and ears, antibacterial teeth, silicone hearts, sheets of skin tissue, elastic bones, and bioengineered ovaries that provide hope for fertility after fighting cancer.

There is also a dark side to 3D printing. Law enforcement is cognizant of the fact that functional 3D printed guns have made their way onto the streets of America. In 2013, over 100,000 blueprints for functioning plastic guns were downloaded from a website before the US government removed the design. Gun enthusiasts have reportedly printed AR-15 lower receivers units, and printed revolvers have been confiscated by the Transportation Safety Administration

(TSA) in carry-on luggage at airports (Hornick, 2017). The concern is growing over the creation of weapons and bombs that could take on the appearance of everyday household consumer products. Sophisticated skimming equipment, printed hands complete with fingerprints, counterfeit watches and handbags are all products of the 3D printing era.

Producing a 3D printed gun.

belekekin/Shutterstock.com

The Mobile Application Ecosystem

As the mobile landscape consisting of smart devices, software, companies, and data transferring processes continues to expand, so does the mobile application ecosystem. According to Statista (2019), mobile applications are projected to continue growing at an exponential rate. In 2018, there were 205.4 billion downloads worldwide, and that number is expected to exceed 258.2 billion by 2022 (see Figure 4.2). Consumers continue to desire convenience and high-quality content on demand at affordable prices.

FIGURE 4.2 Number of mobile app downloads worldwide in 2017, 2018, and 2022 (in billions)

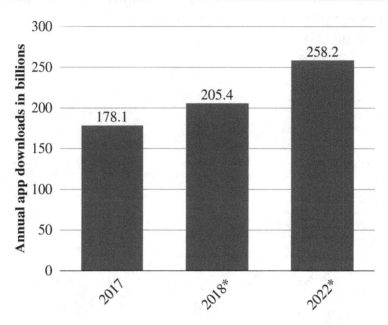

According to SAGipl, an Indian-based mobile and application developer, the most consistently used mobile applications in the world include Facebook, Instagram, Snapchat, Uber, YouTube, Bitmoji, Google Search, Gmail, iCloud, Amazon Mobile, Twitter, Netflix, Pinterest, and WhatsApp (SAGipl, 2019). For US consumers specifically, you can add Airbnb, Spotify, Dropbox, and Grubhub to the list (Singh, 2019). Games such as *Fortnite* and the *Candy Crush* series have been excluded from the list, due to the fact that mobile video games tend to experience very short life cycles.

TikTok, a Chinese video-sharing social networking service owned by ByteDance, has been downloaded over two billion times, ranking it as one of the topmost downloaded apps in Apple's iOS Store (Rouse, 2019). In the first quarter of 2020, TikTok was adding 100 million users per month and was being downloaded more often than Facebook, Instagram, and WhatsApp (see Figure 4.3).

FIGURE 4.3 In the first quarter of 2020, TikTok was adding 100 million users per month and was downloaded more often that Facebook, Instagram, and WhatsApp.

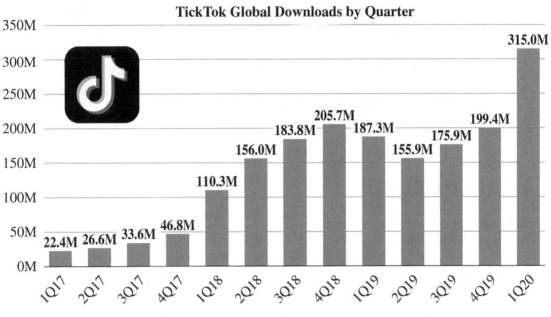

TickTok Global Downloads by Quarter

Compared to other parts of the world, there are mobile apps that are both figuratively and literally foreign to US users. While teaching an international study course in China and Hong Kong, I learned an interesting difference between the ways in which the United States and Mainland China differ in using mobile "apps." In the United States, we use a variety of individual apps such as Bing, Lyft, Google Pay, and Apple Pay to serve our needs. Each app generally tends to operate independently, and consumers switch between apps throughout the day as needed. In China, WeChat is the all-in-one choice for the majority. Developed by Chinese tech giant Tencent, part of the BAT conglomerate (Baidu and Alibaba are two others), WeChat provides users the ability to do many things within one application. In addition to texting, emailing, and making free audio and video calls, WeChat allows users to pick a healthcare professional and schedule appointments, hail a cab, play games, and even provides a digital version of government-issued identification cards. The ID can be used at hotels and airports as a valid form of identification.

The other interesting thing that I noticed was that many Chinese do not carry physical wallets—they use their mobile wallets. WeChat's partnership with Alipay now makes it easy for users to make payments for almost anything. Whether taking public transportation like the train, purchasing clothing, enjoying a tea house or noodle stand, passing a toll booth, managing investments, or paying a utility bill, WeChat offers the ability to pay using a QR (quick response) code for the transaction. After a few weeks in China, I found myself in the rhythm of using WeChat to buy dragon fruit from local street vendors and Star Wars collectibles from small retail shops. It took me a few days to get used to "swiping mode" again when I returned stateside.

Gamification

One final trend that I would like to touch on is gamification, also known as human-centered design. I had the opportunity to speak with Yu-Kai Chou, a thought leader in the space of gamification, and he was passionate about the high level of effectiveness that game-style learning activities are having on real-world outcomes (Chou, 2019). **Gamification** is the "craft of deriving fun and engaging elements typically found in games and thoughtfully applying them to real-work or productive activities" (Chou, 2017, p. 8). Adaptive learning companies are leveraging the technology in their Learning Management Systems (LMSs) for higher education; Fortune 100 companies are using it for training and development; and the U.S. Armed Forces is using it for recruitment activities.

> **Gamification:** The process of adding games or gamelike elements to something (such as a task) so as to encourage participation.

Consider the following: the majority of generational cohorts currently working together in the workplace have been raised playing games on their smartphones and video game systems—they are accustomed to the philosophy and rewards that come with incremental progress (Aguas, 2018). They have been imprinted with a gamification mindset and operate comfortably, if not better, in environments that provide rewards for achievement. The difficulty of any task—no matter how complex—is offset by the sense of learner achievement. Gamification creates a friendly, competitive environment that promotes behavioral change through motivation. As learners advance through the course and take action, their behavior is influenced toward organizational objectives (Pandey, 2017). Credits earned through merit badges can be used toward something as simple as bragging rights, an incentive bonus, or as credit toward insurance premiums, for example. In the process, increased levels of engagement lead to higher employee retention as new expectations are set, and organizational culture is reinforced (Hein, 2013).

Companies like Ei Design use the following key elements to craft a gamification strategy for their clients:

- Challenges (mapping to learning objectives)
- Levels (learning path)
- Instant feedback (to aid progress)
- Scores or points (to impart a sense of accomplishment and gratification)
- Badges (for significant achievements)
- Leaderboards (for analytics)
- Competition (to assess where the learner stands against peers)
- Collaboration (when multiple teams play)

Gamification mechanism

Organizations are integrating gamification into their routine training and delivery operations as well as into programs that educate employees on areas like health and wellness, and compliance. Retail establishments use it as an entertaining activity to measure line management and use it as a metric to determine bonus incentives. In education, the "gamification revolution" is encouraging social connection, reflection, and consistency in both face-to-face and virtual classrooms while auto dealerships leverage gamification to help their sales teams become more familiar with company models and services. Call centers promote competition, creativity, and performance through the gamification of customer interactions (Playvox, 2018) and use the data collected to understand customer and employee pain points and perceptions. A colleague of mine recently completed a gamification course in first aid and safety and was ecstatic to print out the final certificate of accomplishment.

There are now a series of apps that incorporate gamification elements to help users better manage their personal and professional lives. Whether it be finance, fitness, or better working habits like taking out the trash, regularly backing up your hard drive, and getting through your daily emails, leveraging gamification may be an attractive option. There are other emerging trends in technology and innovation, albeit early in their life cycle, but still considered growing contributors to the megatrend nonetheless. Blockchain technology, human augmentation, aerospace technologies, new developments in cybersecurity, and the **democratization of technology** are all gaining momentum in their respective space as they begin defining their roles in reshaping how we live our lives.

> **Democratization of Technology:** The process by which access to technology rapidly continues to become more accessible to more people.

Sergey Nivens/Shutterstock.com

Discussion Questions

1. Who will bear the burden of automation? How will automation affect the supply of labor? How will automation affect wages, and how will wages affect automation? How will automation change job searching?

2. How might research on improving artificial intelligence in robots teach us more about ourselves? Assuming that robots will likely replace most low-complexity jobs, what kind of impact will a mature robotics industry have on the environment?

3. Robotic-arm assisted surgeries are more common now than ever before. If robots assist in performing heart surgery and knee replacements, what is the future of surgical robots? Provide examples.

4. What are the barriers to adopting 3D printing? Why do you consider them obstacles? What is the future of 3D printing? Provide specific examples and explain your position.

5. Define blockchain technology and human augmentation. Provide specific examples of each and explain how they each are shaping the way we live, personally and professionally.

References

Aguas, M. J. (2018, October 5). *The rise of Generation Z* [Paper presentation]. Annual Conference of the Christian Business Faculty Association. Chattanooga, TN, United States.

Amazon. (n.d.). *What robots do (and don't do) at Amazon fulfillment centers.* Retrieved from https://www.aboutamazon.com/amazon-fulfillment/our-innovation/what-robots-do-and-dont-do-at-amazon-fulfillment-centers/

Arnold Machine. (2020). *6 exciting advances in manufacturing automation.* Retrieved from https://www.arnoldmachine.com/6-exciting-advances-manufacturing-automation/

BitcoinPlug. (2020*). Buy Bitcoin in Los Angeles at one of our local ATMs.* Retrieved from https://bitcoinplug.com/

Boulton, C. (2018, September 3). What is RPA? A revolution in business process automation. *CIO.* Retrieved from https://www.cio.com/article/3236451/what-is-rpa-robotic-process-automation-explained.html

Cardpool. (2020). *Welcome to the gift card exchange.* Retrieved from https://www.cardpool.com/

Chou, Y. (2019, April 5). *Actionable gamification* [Conference session]. Crowell School of Business Redemptive Forum, Biola University, La Mirada, CA.

Chou, Y. (2017). *Actionable gamification: Beyond points, badges, and leaderboards.* Octalysis Media.

Crowe, S. (2018, August 7). Ford adding EksoVest exoskeletons to 15 automotive plants. *The Robot Report.* Retrieved from https://www.therobotreport.com/ford-eksovest-exoskeletons-automotive/

ecoATM. (2019). *Instant cash for phones.* Retrieved from https://www.ecoatm.com/

Friedman, T. (2017, August 2). *Thomas Friedman at Aspen* [Video]. YouTube. Retrieved from https://youtu.be/GyZHySRUKXI

Gerber, R. (2019, February 20). Three big tech trends for 2019. *Forbes.* Retrieved from https://www.forbes.com/sites/greatspeculations/2019/02/20/three-big-tech-trends-for-2019/#44adbe2e53eb

Getzoff, M. (2020, January 17). Most technologically advanced countries in the world 2020. *Global Finance.* Retrieved from https://www.gfmag.com/global-data/non-economic-data/best-tech-countries

Gregory, A. S. (2018, September 18). Robotic exoskeletons: The current pros and cons. *World Journal of Orthopedics, 9*(9), 112–119.

Hansen Robotics. (n.d.). *Sophia.* Retrieved from https://www.hansonrobotics.com/sophia/

Hein, R. (2013, June 6). How to use gamification to engage employees. *CIO.* Retrieved from https://www.cio.com/article/2453330/how-to-use-gamification-to-engage-employees.html

Herbert, M. (2017, November 16). 4 ways robots will lead ocean exploration. *The American Society of Mechanical Engineers.* Retrieved from https://www.asme.org/topics-resources/content/4-ways-robots-lead-ocean-exploration

Hornick, J. (2017, February 27). 3D printing and law enforcement. *Corrections.com.* Retrieved from http://www.corrections.com/news/article/45465-3d-printing-and-law-enforcement

Javelin Technologies. (2019). *Industry solutions: 3D design and manufacturing solutions for your industry.* Retrieved from https://www.javelin-tech.com/3d/industry/

Kuepper, J. (2019, July 29). What is a developing country? *The Balance.* Retrieved from https://www.thebalance.com/what-is-a-developing-country-1978982

Leapfrog. (n.d.). *3D printing: How can it improve the medical industry?* Retrieved from https://www.lpfrg.com/blog/3d-printing-in-the-medical-industry/

Martinez, R. (2019, October 17–20). *Surviving the near future: When technological innovation outpaces human adaptation* [Conference session]. Christian Business Faculty Association, Siloam Springs, AR, United States.

Mathis, R. L., Jackson, J. H., Valentine, S. R., & Meglich, P. A. (2017). *Human resource management* (15th ed.). Cengage.

Morikawa, M. (2017). Firms' expectations about the impact of AI and robotics: Evidence from a survey. *Economic Inquiry, 55*(2), 1054–1063.

Morrison, R. (2020, March 9). US Navy is deploying robot submarines controlled by artificial intelligence that could be given the 'power to kill' without any human input. *MailOnline.* Retrieved from https://www.dailymail.co.uk/sciencetech/article-8091685/US-Navy-developing-robot-submarines-controlled-Artificial-Intelligence.html

National Bureau of Economic Research. (2008). *The NBER's recession dating procedure.* Retrieved from http://www.nber.org/cycles/jan08bcdc_memo.html

New Story. (2018, March 12). *New Story + ICON: 3D printed homes for the developing world.* [Video]. YouTube. Retrieved from https://www.youtube.com/watch?v=SvM7jFZGAec

New Story. (2019). *The world's first 3D printed community of printed homes.* Retrieved from https://newstorycharity.org/3d-community/

Nicastro, D. (2018, March 12). 7 ways artificial intelligence is reinventing human resources. *CMSWIRE.* Retrieved from https://www.cmswire.com/digital-workplace/7-ways-artificial-intelligence-is-reinventing-human-resources/

Owen-Hill, A. (2017, June 28). What's the difference between automation and robotics? *Robotiq.* Retrieved from https://blog.robotiq.com/whats-the-difference-between-automation-and-robotics

Pandey, A. (2017, October 24). 5 killer examples on how gamification in the workplace is reshaping corporate training. *eLearning Industry.* Retrieved from https://elearningindustry.com/gamification-in-the-workplace-reshaping-corporate-training-5-killer-examples

Playvox. (2018, June 7). *How to gamify your call center to keep agents motivated.* Retrieved from https://blog.playvox.com/how-to-gamify-your-call-center-to-keep-agents-motivated

RockitCoin. (2019). *Buy & sell Bitcoin.* Retrieved from https://www.rockitcoin.com

Rouse, I. (2019, November 18). TikTok has been downloaded 1.5 billion times. *Hypebeast.* Retrieved from https://hypebeast.com/2019/11/tiktok-downloaded-1-5-billion-times-instagram

SAGipl. (2019). *Most used apps in the world.* Retrieved from https://blog.sagipl.com/most-used-apps/#

Sculpteo. (2019). *3D printers and 3D printing: Technologies, processes and techniques.* Retrieved from https://www.sculpteo.com/en/3d-printing/3d-printing-technologies/

Singh, A. (2019, May 30). Top 10 most popular apps 2019. *Net Solutions.* Retrieved from https://www.netsolutions.com/insights/top-10-most-popular-apps-2018/

Srivastava, S. (2017, September 9). Why RPA implementations fail. *CIO.* Retrieved from https://www.cio.com/article/3226387/why-rpa-implementations-fail.html

Statista. (2019). *Number of mobile app downloads worldwide in 2017, 2018, 2022 (in billions).* Retrieved from https://www.statista.com/statistics/271644/worldwide-free-and-paid-mobile-app-store-downloads/

Technavio. (2019, February 8). *Top mobile payment companies leading the global market payment in 2019.* Retrieved from https://blog.technavio.com/blog/mobile-payment-companies-top-10

The Garage. (2019, March 21). *How 3D printing is transforming lives with better fitting, and better looking, prosthetics.* Retrieved from https://garage.ext.hp.com/us/en/innovation/hp-3d-printing-prosthetics.html

World Health Organization (WHO). (2005). *Guidelines for training personnel in developing countries for prosthetics and orthotics services.* Retrieved from https://cdn.ymaws.com/www.ispoint.org/resource/resmgr/docs/ispo-who_training_guidelines.pdf

Zichermann, G., & Linder, J. (2013). *The gamification revolution: How leaders leverage game mechanics to crush the competition.* McGraw-Hill.

Chapter 5

Globalization

Pasko Maksim/Shutterstock.com

Globalization is defined as the "socioeconomic reform process of eliminating trade, investment, information, technology, cultural and political barriers across countries, which in turn leads to increased economic growth and geopolitical integration and interdependence among nations of the world" (Gaspar et al., 2017, p. 5). Simply put, globalization is the increased interdependence between nations that allows the free flow of goods and services between countries (Northouse, 2019). As political, economic, sociocultural, technological, and legal borders come down, the thinking, attitudes, and behaviors of the global community are led toward working together synergistically (Adler, 2001; Festin, 2001). Advancements in communication systems, transportation, and greater international trade are shrinking the world into one integrated and interconnected global economy.

> **Globalization:** The socioeconomic reform process of eliminating trade, investment, information, technology, cultural and political barriers across countries, which in turn leads to increased economic growth and geopolitical integration and interdependence among nations of the world.

To better understand the impact that globalization has had on our lives, let's consider an example. Picture yourself at your favorite café or restaurant. As you enjoy the benefits of modern amenities and the inviting ambiance, take a look around you. That hot beverage that you are drinking may have come from non-GMO (genetically modified organisms), high-altitude coffee bean plantations in the mountainous region of Loja, Ecuador or from white tea leaves harvested in Jianyang or Songxi counties in the Fujian Province in China. The chocolate almond biscotti may have made its way to your Israeli cut-resistant disposable plate via a small, family-owned business in Northern Italy. Sunlight is diffused through sheer Chinese curtains and complements the mood lighting provided by natural salt lamps made in Pakistan and dimmable backlit mirrors transported from a Canadian distribution center.

In another example, you may be watching a "do-it-yourself" video on how to assemble your Swedish gaming desk while listening to an American media streaming service, all while wearing jeans made in Mexico and a T-shirt made with Indian cotton transported from Hong Kong in a standard 40-foot ISO container by a Japanese shipping company. Finally, take a good look at that smart device you have been glued to. It was assembled mostly in China with parts from Taiwan, Singapore, South Korea, France, Italy, and the Netherlands.

An increasing number of domestic and international companies practicing globalization, as well as smaller and mid-sized organizations, are also reaping the benefits of flatter, more egalitarian structures as compared to taller options with layers of hierarchy—this construct is known as **decentralization**. Modeled by early railroad companies in the United States (Broekstra, 2014), decentralization empowers decision making as low on the chain of command as possible. For example, the decentralized authority could be given to the North American division of a European auto manufacturer, a regional office of a national fast-food chain, or a manager of a suburban franchise. Where appropriate, decentralization increases flexibility and speed in the decision-making and execution process. Decentralized locations can adapt quickly to the changing landscape, minimizing bureaucratic red tape. As global organizations rely on local insight to pinpoint strengths and weaknesses, employees develop specialized expertise increasing intellectual capital and employee morale, all while mitigating large-scale centralized errors (GoCo, 2020).

> **Decentralization:** A type of organizational structure in which daily operations and decision-making responsibilities are delegated away from a central authoritative location or group to lower level managers, geographic locales, or product and service segments.

A corporate video conference with management team members located throughout the world.

Mega conglomerates like Johnson & Johnson have adopted a decentralized management approach that has allowed its 250 subsidiary companies with operations in 60 countries to flourish under three decentralized segments: Consumer, Pharmaceutical and Medical Devices, and Diagnostics (Johnson & Johnson, 2015). Many global nonprofits have also found that adhering to local models has been more efficient than relying on a centralized approach. Financial institutions in the United States tend to operate on the other side of the spectrum—highly centralized partly due to regulation by government agencies such as:

- The Federal Reserve Board (FRB, "The Fed")
- The Federal Deposit Insurance Company (FDIC)
- The Office of the Comptroller of the Currency (OCC)
- The Commodity Futures Trading Commission (CFTC)
- The Securities and Exchange Commission (SEC)
- The Consumer Financial Protection Bureau (CFPB)

> **Blockchain:** A decentralized method of peer-to-peer recordkeeping using numerous computers working together simultaneously and in concert, to produce a distributed or shared ledger through a consensus of algorithms (Casey, 2020).

Blockchain technology may present a future solution to the DeFi (decentralized finance) movement; however, for now, many of the larger financial institutions remain centralized.

Decentralization fuels innovation, accountability (for subunit performance), speed, efficiency, and effectiveness. In the right circumstances, empowering narrow geographic, operational, and/or product line segments can increase a company's distinctive competence in the marketplace. At worst, decentralization can cause delays in critical communication, role redundancy, a departure from corporate objectives and vision, silo-thinking, and a lack of collaboration. I am finding that a growing number of organizations today are utilizing a hybrid or blended approach to their operations, combining both centralized and decentralized elements.

> **Maquiladora:** A light-assembly manufacturing operation or factory (aka twin plant) in Mexico, usually near the U.S.-Mexico border, that operates under a favorable duty or tariff-free basis— the parent company is located in the United States.

Globalization is benefiting the United States in its role as a megatrend in many forms. In one way, it is providing American-owned businesses with low-cost workforce options in developing nations. The **maquiladora** corridor in Northern Mexico, for example, produces everything from clothing and consumer electronics to cars, drones, medical devices, and aircraft components. Materials, production equipment, and assembly components are sent to Mexico by the American-owned parent company, assembled at the maquiladora, and then exported back to the United States. This production scheme operates under special programs that grant tax breaks while optimizing transportation costs and turnaround times. From 2007 to 2020, maquiladora workers earned $2.40 per hour compared to the $15 to $40 range paid for skilled manufacturing labor in the United States (Trading Economics, 2020). Along with these significant savings in labor costs, Mexico's growing labor force has matured and is producing a more capable worker with the technical skills required to manufacture higher-quality products. Finally, the maquiladora industry has helped in reducing the trade risk between the United States and Mexico—less trade disrupted translates to more productivity (Acrecent Financial Corporation, 2020).

Multinational companies like Exxon Mobil, Hilton, UnitedHealthcare Global, and organizations like the Red Cross operate 24 hours a day, responding swiftly through an extensive network of satellite offices and branches around the globe. Global news networks like CNN and Fox News contribute to the spread of knowledge almost instantaneously while tourism allows for the exchange of money, culture, and ideas. In my lifetime, it's been amazing to see the amount of influence that American culture has had on the rest of the world—music, fashion, technology, sports. In fact, I found it interesting to learn that the term "McWorld" is commonly used to describe both the "McDonaldization" of the American fast-food company as well as a general descriptor of the effects of American internationalization of goods and services on indigenous cultures.

McDonalds location in Moscow.

The internationalization of the United States is also vividly apparent through the processes of free trade, outsourcing, the exportation of American culture, and immigration. Communications technology (the Internet, telecommunications, broadband, and wireless smart devices) allows geographically dispersed workers to interact and collaborate as though they were all in the same location (Chestnut, 2019)—**supranationalism** at its finest.

> **Supranational:** Beyond the borders or scope of any one nation.

The Resurgence of Globalization in the United States

Globalization has been driven by the global expansion of multinational corporations based in the United States and Europe, as well as the worldwide exchange of new developments in science, technology, and products. After experiencing a breakdown at the beginning of the 20th century in tandem with World War I (1914–1918), the United States began experiencing a resurgence in globalization Post-World War II as eight million men and women stationed abroad began demobilizing back to the United States. At the time, there were 12 million men and women serving in the Armed Forces, thus 75% were returning home after serving abroad. All in, there were 16 million men and women that had served in the armed forces during World War II (Kohn, 2016). As the "Silent Generation" returned home, they reentered the civilian workforce and began accumulating wealth, demanding higher-quality products at competitive prices. Foreign goods quickly began flooding the US market.

A series of key events also contributed to the surge in globalization in the United States in the early 20th century. At the height of the Great Depression, Franklin Delano Roosevelt was inaugurated as the 32nd president of the United States in 1933. As the new administration moved into power, it realized that farms and factories that had been stimulated during World War I were producing material on over 40 million acres of land, which could not be consumed within the country (Wallace, 1934). This opened world markets and offered an opportunity for expanding trade. The Bretton Woods Conference in 1944 led to an agreement by major governments around the world to establish the framework for international monetary policy, commerce, and finance. The General Agreement on Tariffs and Trade (GATT), signed by its first 23 nations on October 30, 1947, helped promote international trade by reducing and eliminating trade barriers, eliminating preferential treatment, and promoting trade on a reciprocal and mutually advantageous basis. The North Atlantic Treaty Organization (NATO) in 1949 was established in the wake of World War II to secure peace in Europe, promote cooperation among its members, and guard their freedom. Rebuilt countries were poised for growth and foreign products began to flood the US market. The focus of US and European multinational companies on worldwide expansion combined with the events above accelerated the pace of globalization.

Perhaps, the most significant, strategic, and diplomatic advancement of the 20th century in globalization occurred during US President Richard Nixon's visit to China in 1972 which cleared the trail to better relations between the two nations, calling for increased trade and travel. Dubbed the "week that changed the world, President Nixon's historic meeting with Chairman Mao led to the Shanghai Communiqué, and later the Joint Communiqué on the Establishment of Diplomatic Relations establishing official relations between the United States and the People's Republic of China that would flourish in the years to come.

President Nixon and Chairman Mao's historic meeting in 1972.
Source: South China Morning Post

Nixon summarized the significance of the meeting between the two countries:

This was the week that changed the world, as what we have said in that Communiqué is not nearly as important as what we will do in the years ahead to build a bridge across 16,000 miles and 22 years of hostilities which have divided us in the past. And what we have said today is that we shall build that bridge (UPI, 1972).

The history of globalization is fascinating—I would recommend a study of the Silk Road, a network of trade routes that connected China and the Far East with the Middle East and Europe. Derived from a lucrative trade in silk carried out along its roads from 130 BC to 1453 AD—until the Ottoman Empire boycotted trade with China and closed the routes—the Silk Road has had a long-lasting impact on commerce, culture, and history that still resonates today (A&E Television, 2019). Trade along the Silk Road economic belt included fruits and vegetables, livestock, grain, leather and hides, tools, religious objects, artwork, precious stones and metals and—perhaps more importantly—language, culture, religious beliefs, philosophy, and science. Commodities such as paper and gunpowder, both invented by the Chinese during the Han Dynasty, had obvious and lasting impacts on culture and history in the West. Rich spices of the East quickly became popular in the West changing cuisine across much of Europe. Techniques for making glass migrated eastward to China from the Islamic world and it was through the Silk Road that opium was likely introduced to China and East Asia in the sixth or seventh century AD.

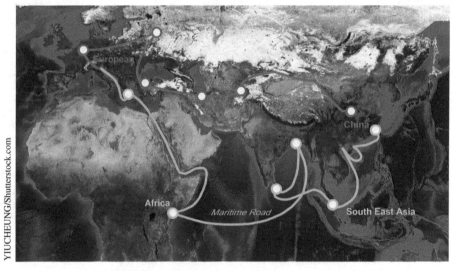

The Silk Road Economic Belt and Maritime Route.

Gross Domestic Product: The total value of final goods and services produced within a nation's borders in a given period of time.

Continuing the journey into contemporary globalization, let's take a look at a list of countries with high levels of GDP, and explore the trading-type relationship they have with the United States. **Gross Domestic Product** is the total value of final goods and services produced within a nation's borders in a given period of time and serves as a monetary measure when comparing living standards between nations. Applying **purchasing power parity (PPP)** levels the playing field by allowing us to compare the absolute purchasing power of a country's currency to measure the prices of specific goods and services. According to the U.S. Central Intelligence Agency (2020), the geographies with the highest GDP in 2017 were China, the European Union (EU), and the United States (see Table 5.1).

> **Purchasing Power Parity (PPP):** Adjusting the exchange rate between countries to ensure that a good is purchased for the same price in the same currency.

TABLE 5.1 Largest Global Economies by GDP (Purchasing Power Parity)

Rank	Country	GDP (Purchasing Power Parity)
1	CHINA	$23,160,000,000,000
2	EUROPEAN UNION	$20,850,000,000,000
3	UNITED STATES	$19,390,000,000,000
4	INDIA	$9,459,000,000,000
5	JAPAN	$5,429,000,000,000
6	GERMANY	$4,171,000,000,000
7	RUSSIA	$4,008,000,000,000
8	INDONESIA	$3,243,000,000,000
9	BRAZIL	$3,240,000,000,000
10	UNITED KINGDOM	$2,914,000,000,000
11	FRANCE	$2,836,000,000,000
12	MEXICO	$2,458,000,000,000
13	ITALY	$2,311,000,000,000
14	TURKEY	$2,173,000,000,000
15	KOREA, SOUTH	$2,029,000,000,000

Source: U.S. Central Intelligence Agency.

Trade Partners and Agreements

The largest global economies also happen to serve as major trading partners with the United States. The United States' main exports to China are civilian aircraft, engines, equipment and parts, followed by semiconductors, optical and medical equipment, and passenger cars (Statista, 2020). Agricultural product exports include soybeans, cotton, hides and skins, pork and pork products, and coarse grains. Leading service exports are in the travel, intellectual property (trademark, computer software), and transport sectors. China, in turn, exports electrical machinery, furniture and bedding, toys and sports gear, and equipment plastics to the United States. Serving as the third largest supplier of agricultural products to the United States, China supplies over $4.9 billion annually in processed fruit and vegetables, fruit and vegetable juices, snack foods, spices, and fresh vegetables. Leading service imports from China are comprised of transport, travel, and research and development sectors (Office of the United States Trade Representative, 2020a).

The European Union, made up of 28 member states that include Germany, France, Italy, Portugal, and Malta, was also formed in the aftermath of World War II, and currently ranks as the United States' top trading partner. Although the United Kingdom (England, Scotland, Wales, and Northern Ireland) formally left the European Union on Brexit day, January 31, 2020, there is still much to navigate in the months ahead during the implementation period, including what the future relationship would look like between the United Kingdom and the European Union. The United States exports aircraft machinery, fuel oil, optical and medical instruments, and pharmaceuticals. Leading categories of agricultural exports include soybeans, tree nuts, wine and beer, and processed food (Office of the United States Trade Representative, 2020b). The United States has an **intraindustry trade** type of relationship with the European Union, meaning that both countries trade goods and services produced in the same industry. For example, the European Union also exports pharmaceuticals, optical and medical equipment, and electrical machinery to the United States—all goods that the United States also exports to the European Union.

> **Intra-industry Trade:** Trade of goods produced in the same industry (between two countries).

Trade of goods and services with India totaled an estimated $142.6 billion in 2018. Exports were $58.7 billion, imports $83.9 billion resulting in a trade deficit with India of $25.2 (Office of the United States Trade Representative, 2020c).

The bilateral trade's top export to India is precious metal and stones (diamonds), mineral fuels, aircraft, machinery, and organic chemicals. Leading agricultural export categories include tree nuts, cotton, fresh fruit, dairy products, and prepared food. United States' exports of services total $25.2 billion and focus on the travel, intellectual property (computer software, audio- and visual-related products), and transport sectors. Similar to other trading partner relationships, top import categories include precious metal and stone (diamonds), pharmaceuticals, machinery, mineral fuels, and vehicles. According to the Office of the United States Trade Representative (2020c), agricultural products from India total $2.7 billion and are comprised of spices, rice, essential oils, processed fruit and vegetables, and other vegetable oils. Leading services imports from India to the United States were in the telecommunications, computer and information services, research and development, and travel sectors.

Loading containers for export at Deendayal Port Trust in the Gulf of Kutch, India.

In its bilateral economic relations with the United States, Japan is both a major trading partner and an international investor. The US—Japan Alliance is the cornerstone of US interests in Asia and "fundamental to regional stability and prosperity" (U.S. Department of State, 2020, p. 1). The countries collaborate in areas such as brain science, aging, infectious disease, personalized medicine, and space exploration as well as in communications technology supply chains. US goods and services trade with Japan totaled an estimated $303.0 billion in 2019. Exports were $123.4 billion; imports were $179.6 billion, resulting in an overall trade deficit with Japan of $56.3 billion (Office of the United States Trade Representative, 2020d). Similar to its trading relationship with other countries, top export categories include mineral fuels, aircraft, optical and medical instruments, machinery, and electrical machinery. Japan is the United States' fourth largest agricultural export market ($12 billion) with corn, beef and beef products, pork and pork products, soybeans, and wheat. The top import categories are vehicles, machinery, electrical machinery, optical and medical instruments, and pharmaceuticals—another example of countries practicing dyadic, intraindustry trade.

It would be a disservice to investigate the trading relationships between the United States and its global partners without a nod to the world's major areas of regional economic integration and cooperation, some of which include the United States as a member (see Table 5.2). The Office of the U.S. Trade Representative (USTR) is responsible for developing and coordinating US international trade, commodity, and direct investment policy, and overseeing negotiations with other countries. American trade policy works toward opening markets throughout the world to create new opportunities and higher living standards for families, farmers,

TABLE 5.2 The Major Areas of Regional Economic Integration

Free Trade Agreements	Members	Summary
The United States—Mexico—Canada Agreement (USMCA), revision of the North American Free Trade Agreement (NAFTA)	United States, Mexico, and Canada	(2018) Strengthening anew the long-standing economic cooperation that has developed through trade and investment. The goal is to create more balanced, reciprocal trade that supports high-paying jobs for Americans and growing the North American economy.

Free Trade Agreements	Members	Summary
The Dominican Republic— Central America Free Trade Agreement (CAFTA-DR)	United States, Costa Rica, the Dominican Republic, El Salvador, Guatemala, Honduras, and Nicaragua	(2004) Promotes stronger trade and investment ties, prosperity, and stability throughout the region and along the United States' Southern border.
The Common Market of the South (MERCOSUR)	Full Members: Argentina, Brazil, Paraguay, and Uruguay Associate Members: Bolivia, Chile, Colombia, Ecuador, Guyana, Peru, and Suriname	(1991) The largest preferential trade agreement in Latin America. Represents 70% of the South American population and 77% of region's total GDP.
Union of South American Nations (USAN or UNASUR)	Argentina, Bolivia, Brazil, Chile, Colombia, Ecuador, Guyana, Paraguay, Peru, Suriname, Uruguay, and Venezuela	(2008) The Andean Community and The Common Market of the South combined to form USAN to build an integration and union among its peoples in the cultural, social, economic and political fields, prioritizing political dialogue, social policies, education, energy, infrastructure, financing and the environment, to strengthen democracy and reduce asymmetries

(*continued*)

Free Trade Agreements	Members	Summary
The Association of Southeast Asian Nations (ASEAN)	Indonesia, Malaysia, the Philippines, Singapore, Thailand Brunei, Vietnam, Laos, Burma, and Cambodia	(1967) Promotes political and economic cooperation, and regional stability. Comprised of three pillars: Political Security Community, Economic Community, and Sociocultural Community.
Asia-Pacific Economic Cooperation (APEC)	United States, Australia, Brunei Darussalam, Canada, Chile, China, Hong Kong, Indonesia; Japan, Malaysia, Mexico, New Zealand, Papua New Guinea, Peru, the Philippines; Russia, Singapore, Republic of Korea, Taiwan (Chinese Taipei), Thailand, and Vietnam	(1989) Forum for facilitating economic growth, cooperation, trade and investment in the Asia-Pacific region. The aim is to create greater prosperity for the people of the region by promoting balanced, inclusive, sustainable, innovative, and secure growth, and by accelerating regional economic integration.
The European Union (EU)	Austria, Belgium, Bulgaria, Croatia, Cyprus, Czech Republic, Denmark, Estonia, Finland, France, Germany, Greece, Hungary, Ireland, Italy, Latvia, Lithuania, Luxembourg, Malta, Netherlands, Poland, Portugal, Romania, Slovakia, Slovenia, Spain, and Sweden	(1993) The United States' trade and investment relationship with the countries of Europe is the largest and most complex in the world. US transatlantic economic ties are dominated by relations with the 28-member European Union (EU).

Free Trade Agreements	Members	Summary
The Gulf Cooperation Council (GCC)	Bahrain, Kuwait, Saudi Arabia, Oman, Qatar, and the United Arab Emirates (UAE)	(1981) The regional intergovernmental political and economic union of six oil-exporting countries of the Persian Gulf. The goal of the GCC is to promote unity across member nations based on common objectives as well as similar political and cultural views.
The African Economic Community (AEC)	All 54 countries on the African Continent	(1991) Establishes grounds for mutual economic development among the majority of African states. Stated goals include the creation of free trade areas, customs unions, a single market, a central bank, and a common currency establishing economic and monetary union.
The Caribbean Community (CARICOM)	Full Members: Antigua and Barbuda, The Bahamas, Barbados, Belize, Dominica, Grenada, Guyana, Haiti, Jamaica, Montserrat, Saint Lucia, Saint Kitts and Nevis, St. Vincent and the Grenadines Suriname, and Trinidad and Tobago Associate Members: Anguilla, Bermuda, British Virgin Islands, Cayman Islands, Turks and Caicos Islands	(1973) Supports a unified Caribbean Community and promotes economic integration and cooperation among its members. Competitive sharing in economic, social, and cultural prosperity.

Source: Jake Aguas.

manufacturers, workers, consumers, and businesses (Office of the United States Trade Representative, 2020e, p. 1).

The USTR is part of the Executive Office of the President and coordinates trade policy, resolves disagreements, and frames issues for presidential decision. The United States currently has agreements in force with 20 countries.

Trade Regulation and Barriers to Entry

Although the past century has experienced a major paradigm shift toward globalization and free trade, governments do intervene using several key policies to regulate and manage trade. Dunung (2020) highlights the following government intervention policy areas:

- Tariff—A tax (duty) imposed on an imported good.
- Subsidy—A form of financial support to assist an industry or business so that the price of a commodity or service may remain low or competitive.
- Import quotas and Voluntary Export Restraints (VERs)—Limitations on the amount of a product that one country is permitted to import/export to another.
- Currency controls—Limiting the convertibility of one currency into others; managing the exchange rate at a high level to create an import disincentive.

Lucia Pitter/Shutterstock.com

- Local content requirements—Requiring that a certain percentage of a product or an item be manufactured or "assembled" locally.
- Antidumping rules—Guidelines preventing companies from selling products below market prices in an effort to win market share and weaken a competitor, a form of predatory behavior.
- Export financing—Providing financing to domestic companies to promote exports.
- Free trade zone—Areas that experience reduced tariffs, taxes, customs, procedures, or restrictions to promote trade with other countries.
- Administrative policies—Bureaucratic policies and procedures governments use to deter imports by making entry or operations more difficult.
- Trade embargo—A government order that restricts commerce with a specified country or the exchange of a specific good.

There are numerous combinations of political, economic, social, and cultural reasons that governments choose to intervene. A country may be seeking to protect producers or industries in domestic markets. It may be attempting to guard its national security (e.g., weapons, aerospace, advanced electronics, strategic minerals) or protect domestic jobs. Finally, government intervention may occur as a retaliatory measure toward countries that are not economically fair or as a reward mechanism for political support on global matters. Globalization also promotes intercultural competence: the ability to interact effectively with individuals of other cultures (Moodian, 2009). Organizations and their leaders are fine-tuning their cultural intelligence through the use of assessment tools and cross-cultural training in an effort to increase their effectiveness across international borders. Leading globally now requires an appreciation for the world's cultural nuances—religious backgrounds, customs, traditions, and languages. Globalization and cultural intelligence are increasing an organization's reach, allowing it to expand its international footprint.

Globalization creates employment opportunities and promotes the improvement of market efficiencies. Consensus and cooperation between countries help reduce barriers to trade and invite the production of higher-quality products at competitive wages. Consistent and fair criteria for foreign investment and trade give countries the opportunity to compete and benefit from free trade. Trade agreements between countries and regions facilitate the production and transportation of goods between member countries in the trading bloc without additional regulations and tariffs.

Globalization also has the opposite effect and can create just as many challenges. As trade agreements and customs unions seek to protect the self-interests of their members, they create a breeding ground for trade diversion, a shifting of exports from a more efficient nonmember to a less efficient member. In the same way, transitioning manufacturing to international labor markets impacts domestic employment and creates a stronger dependence on foreign support. Shortages caused by the COVID-19 outbreak revealed just how globally reliant the United States had become on its foreign partners for medical supplies such as N95 respirator masks, saline bags, and prescription pain relievers. In fact, current legislative efforts are being developed to curtail and altogether prevent placing the United States in such predicaments in the future. According to Gerhart (personal communication, 2020) there has been a:

> "growing disaffection with globalism in some quarters of the United States Social media is replete with a whole conservative subculture that spits out the word *globalist* as a pejorative. Much of this sentiment seems to be rooted in ignoble ignorance and unfettered ethnocentrism, but it is real nonetheless."

Manufacturers around the United States have had to also deal with intense foreign competition over the years as international options have become more readily available at competitive prices. In response, companies have had to reduce their costs, reduce their pricing, relocate, or close down altogether. Many have also had to find other avenues of revenue to survive. The decline of domestic job opportunities and revenue, cyclical crises, nontariff barriers to trade, the spread of pandemics, and new security issues have all contributed to a challenging landscape (Baffour Awuah & Amal, 2011). Even with these disruptions, it is impossible to escape globalization or enjoy the benefits that come with membership to the "global village."

PopTika/Shutterstock.com

Travel mania/Shutterstock.com

Discussion Questions

1. Has globalization gone too far, not far enough, or has it been heading in the wrong direction? Explain and provide specific examples to support your position.

2. Do you think it would be a good idea if all barriers to trade were removed from the world and people could freely export and import without customs duties or any other problems? What impact would such a change have? Discuss three pros and three cons.

3. Identify a US-owned company that operates a maquiladora in Mexico? Discuss the history of the shift and reasons why the company moved its operations to Mexico. Discuss the specific benefits and challenges it is currently facing as a result.

4. What are the significant differences between the United States—Mexico—Canada Agreement (USMCA) and its predecessor, the North American Free Trade Agreement (NAFTA)? Could the new regional content rules disrupt supply chains in North America? Explain.

5. Challenge yourself beyond the scope of material in this chapter by research-
   ing the four basic levels of international activity: Domestic business, International business, Multinational business, and Global business. Define each
   of the four levels and emphasize the specific differences between them. Provide an example of a company for each level and explain why it aligns with
   that level.

References

Acrecent Financial Corporation. (2020). *The benefits of setting up maquiladoras in
Mexico, such as lower production costs, outweigh the hurdles.* Retrieved from
https://www.acrecent.com/maquiladoras-in-mexico-benefits-and-challenges/

Adler, N. (2001). Global leadership: Women leaders. In M. Mendenhall, T. M.
Kuhlmann, & G. Stahl (Eds.), *Developing global business leaders: Policies,
processes, and innovations* (pp. 73–97). Quorum.

A&E Television. (2019, September 26). Silk road. *History.com.* Retrieved from
https://www.history.com/topics/ancient-middle-east/silk-road

Baffour Awuah, G., & Amal, M. (2011). Impact of globalization. *European
Business Review, 23*(1), 120–132.

Broekstra, G. (2014). *Building high-performance, high-trust organizations:
Decentralization 2.0.* Palgrave MacMillan.

Casey, M. (2020, February 1). *What is blockchain?* [Video]. Investopedia.
Retrieved from https://www.investopedia.com/terms/b/blockchain.asp

Chestnut, D. (2019, January 25). Globalization & communication technology.
Bizfluent. Retrieved from https://bizfluent.com/about-6773168-globalization-
communication-technology.html

Dunung, S. P. (2020). *Global business management.* Flatworld.

Festin, M. (2001) The effects of international human resource management
strategies on global leadership development. In M. Mendenhall, T. M.
Kuhlmann, & G. Stahl (Eds.), *Developing global business leaders: policies,
processes, and innovations* (pp. 37–56). Quorum.

Gaspar, J. E., Arreola-Risa, A., Bierman, L., Hise, R. T., Kolari, J. W., & Smith,
L. M. (2017). *Introduction to globalization* (2nd ed.). McGraw-Hill.

GoCo. (2020). *The rise of the decentralized organization*. Retrieved from https://www.goco.io/blog/rise-decentralized-organization/

Johnson & Johnson. (2015). *Annual report*. Retrieved from https://web.archive.org/web/20160418084123/http://files.shareholder.com/downloads/JNJ/1709744668x0x881109/474857DD-8E67-43B1-BB38-0A9712D93545/2015_annual_report_.pdf

Kohn, A. (2016, May 8). It's amazing just how many Americans served in World War II. *Timeline*. Retrieved from https://timeline.com/its-amazing-just-how-many-americans-served-in-world-war-ii-18d197a685ca

Moodian, M. A. (2009). *Contemporary leadership and cultural competence: Exploring the cross-cultural dynamics within organizations*. Sage.

Northouse, P. G. (2019). *Leadership: Theory and practice* (8th ed.). Sage.

Office of the United States Trade Representative. (2020a). *The People's Republic of China: U.S.-China trade facts*. Retrieved from https://ustr.gov/countries-regions/china-mongolia-taiwan/peoples-republic-china

Office of the United States Trade Representative. (2020b). *European Union*. Retrieved from https://ustr.gov/countries-regions/europe-middle-east/europe/european-union

Office of the United States Trade Representative. (2020c). *U.S.-India trade investment*. Retrieved from https://ustr.gov/countries-regions/south-central-asia/india

Office of the United States Trade Representative. (2020d). *Japan*. Retrieved from https://ustr.gov/countries-regions/japan-korea-apec/japan

Office of the United States Trade Representative. (2020e). *Mission of the USTR*. Retrieved from https://ustr.gov/about-us/about-ustr

Statista. (2020). *Value of exported goods from the United States to China in 2019, by commodity category*. Retrieved from https://www.statista.com/statistics/354498/us-leading-export-categories-to-china/

Trading Economics. (2020). *Mexico nominal hourly wages in manufacturing 2007–2020*. Retrieved from https://tradingeconomics.com/mexico/wages-in-manufacturing

UPI. (1972). *1972 year in review: Nixon goes to China*. Retrieved from https://www.upi.com/Archives/Audio/Events-of-1972/Nixon-Goes-to-China/?spt=nil&d=n

U.S. Central Intelligence Agency. (2020). Country comparison: GDP (PPP). *World Factbook.* Retrieved from https://www.cia.gov/library/publications/the-world-factbook/rankorder/2001rank.html

U.S. Department of State. (2020, January 21). U.S. relations with Japan. *Bureau of East Asian and Pacific Affairs.* Retrieved from https://www.state.gov/u-s-relations-with-japan/

Wallace, H. A. (1934, January). American agriculture and world markets. *Foreign Affairs.* Retrieved from https://www.foreignaffairs.com/articles/united-states/1934-01-01/american-agriculture-and-world-markets

Chapter 6

The World Wide Web and the Internet

sdecoret/Shutterstock.com

I n less than 30 years, the United States has become highly interdependent on **the World Wide Web** and **the Internet**. Users rely on these resources for their livelihood—information, work, communication, health, relationships, finances, shopping, education, entertainment, self-expression, and help. Weber (2011) suggests that the Internet has changed our lives and that people are spending more hours on the Internet, the longer they have been using it. This, in turn, is contributing to behavioral addiction and an unhealthy reliance on this communication technology. Data from the Center for the Digital Future at USC Annenberg (2018) suggests 92% of Americans are Internet users and that the average American spends 13.5% of their week (22.5 hours) online—emailing, texting,

The World Wide Web (WWW): a system of extensively interlinked hypertext documents; a branch of the Internet.

The Internet: a vast computer network linking smaller computer networks worldwide.

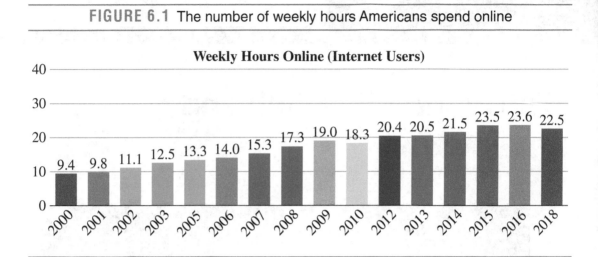

FIGURE 6.1 The number of weekly hours Americans spend online

and using social media and other forms of communication. Figure 6.1 illustrates the incremental increase of usage in hours per week since 2000.

Connection to the World Wide Web comes in many forms: smart devices (mobile phones, tablets, and watches), laptops and personal computers, game consoles, home networks, digital video recorders (DVRs), and devices connecting the Internet to televisions. In this chapter, we will delve into the evolution of the megatrend known as "the Web" while exploring its relationship with the Internet.

The Evolution of the World Wide Web

I remember my first experience with the Web and Internet. I was working for a market research company in Santa Monica, California and had been comfortable interacting with the organization's central network—adding, removing, and working off files within the construct of our onsite systems. One day, the director of Information Technology (IT) walked into my office and said that he was going to open my eyes to a larger world and asked me to step away from my desk for a few moments. He sat down and began tapping away at the keyboard as if he were playing a rendition of Beethoven's Für Elise and when he was done, he jumped up and said, "You're in!" I asked, "In what?" He sat me down and asked me to type in an odd sequence of characters that started with "www" followed by a company name and a ".com" The next thing I knew, we were connected to a Fortune 100 company's website—a glamorous one-page website at the time, that only listed the company address, motto, and logo. By that day's standard, the small activity was historic for me. Slightly realizing and understanding what had just happened, I looked at him in amazement. "You are now part of the Internet, the world wide web—your life will never be the same" (IT Director, personal communication, Year), he said. How right he was.

Characterized by static websites that really did not change once created, Web 1.0 was considered the first stage of development with little user functionality, if any. The "information web" provided users with static, read-only information about individuals, companies, and organizations. Producer-generated web pages were informative but did not provide visitors with an incentive to come back to the site after the initial visit—examples include early versions of personal and company websites.

> **Web 1.0:** The first stage of development of the World Wide Web that was characterized by simple static websites.

According to Strickland (2008), Web 1.0 sites were noninteractive and applications were proprietary, meaning that visitors could download them but not necessarily see how the application worked or made modifications—they were closed-source programs where code was neither published nor shared with the public. Tim Berners-Lee is credited as the inventor of the World Wide Web project

World Wide Web

The WorldWideWeb (W3) is a wide-area hypermedia information retrieval initiative aiming to give universal access to a large universe of documents.

Everything there is online about W3 is linked directly or indirectly to this document, including an executive summary of the project, Mailing lists , Policy , November's W3 news , Frequently Asked Questions .

What's out there?
        Pointers to the world's online information, subjects , W3 servers, etc.
Help
        on the browser you are using
Software Products
        A list of W3 project components and their current state.
        (e.g. Line Mode ,X11 Viola , NeXTStep , Servers , Tools , Mail robot , Library)
Technical
        Details of protocols, formats, program internals etc
Bibliography
        Paper documentation on W3 and references.
People
        A list of some people involved in the project.
History
        A summary of the history of the project.
How can I help ?
        If you would like to support the web..
Getting code
        Getting the code by anonymous FTP , etc.

"The first-ever website and computer used to create the World Wide Web (WWW)."

SSPL/Getty Images

Science & Society Picture Library/SSPL/Getty Images

and posted the first website that described the web and how to use it on August 6, 1991 while at CERN, the European Organization for Nuclear Research (Shontell, 2011). The project's name, World Wide Web, was renamed Nexus to differentiate it from the actual World Wide Web and served as the only browser and access point to the web at the time (McPeak, 2018).

Berners-Lee had proposed a solution to the challenges he had been facing in trying to keep track of the volume of projects and computer systems that thousands of researchers had been working on across the organization and across the globe. He found it inefficient having to learn different programs on different computers systems to get the information he needed. Using **hypertext** to link documents on different computer systems, Berners-Lee developed the substratum of the Web including Hypertext Markup Language (HTML) for creating web pages, Hypertext Transfer Protocol (HTTP) for transferring data across the web, and Uniform Resource Locators (URLs) that served as web addresses for locating documents and pages (Nix, 2018).

> **Hypertext:** The ability to access information related to a topic and graphic by a point-and-click method.

In 1993, the University of Illinois' National Center for Supercomputing Applications released Mosaic, the first **Web browser** to become popular with the general public. Since then, Internet Explorer (1995), Mozilla Firefox (2002), Apple Safari (2003), Google Chrome (2008), Microsoft Bing (2009), and Microsoft Edge (2015) have all gained market adoption and become the standard. In 2016, a consortium of Chinese companies led by Qihoo 360 Technology Company purchased Opera, a chromium-based browser for $600 million from a Norwegian company.

> **Web Browser:** A software program that allows a user to locate, access, and display web pages

Once a popular **search engine** in China, search services offered by Google were blocked by the Great Firewall in the People's Republic of China on March 30, 2010. In less than 4 years, Google's search market share in China had declined from 36.2% in 2009 to less than 2% in 2013 (Carsten, 2013). Chinese-owned search engine Baidu (baidu.com) has now become the second-largest search engine in the world, holding over 65% market share in China's search engine market compared to its domestic contender, Sogou (sogou.com) which controls 18% (Sun, 2020).

> **Search Engine:** a site on the World Wide Web that is used to search data (such as text and images) for specified information and providing a list of documents in which they are found.

With over 90 million users, the largest Internet market in Europe belongs to Russia (Melkadze, 2019), where Google plays second fiddle to Yandex (Yandex.ru) in the web search engine market. According to Schwartz (2014), Russia's Yandex distinguishes itself from Google's search engine with five distinct advantages:

- Yandex serves as a portal to the largest media destination—for many Russians, Yandex is where they begin and end their day
- Yandex is better suited for Russian language searches; Google is not as effective
- The Android mobile operating system controls over 70% of the Russian mobile market (Liu, 2019); Yandex has captured 52% of the search market on Android devices.
- Russians have an affinity toward Russian brands, likely increasing its use
- Yandex algorithms are better suited to account for spam

Web 2.0, also known as the "social web" and "participative web," enhanced the online experience by emphasizing user interaction with the Internet, all while harnessing the power of collective intelligence. Coined by DiNucci (1999), the term Web 2.0 was devised to differentiate the post-dotcom bubble World Wide Web from that which came before (Hosch, 2017). The 2.0 appellation represents the birth of social media, a time characterized by social networking, user-driven content, and cloud computing. In this open-source platform, users send messages, provide feedback, offer solutions, apply for open job postings, order products, contribute to blogs, and even donate to support an organization's social responsibility efforts. Video game companies provide gamers with "mods," the ability to modify and alter characters and environments, creating new scenarios and behaviors adding to the depth of the original work. This has led to the emergence and rise in artistic game modification, machinima, and demoscene, extending the life cycle of video game sales.

In the heart of this revolution in modern communication lies a deluge of social media platforms and sites that provide a medium of connecting with others who share similar personal or career interests. Consumers, companies,

> **Web 2.0:** The second stage of the World Wide Web that emphasizes social networking, user-generated content, cloud computing, and enhanced interoperability.

> **Social networking:** Building social relationships with other people who share similar personal or career interests, activities, backgrounds or real-life connections through an online platform.

> **Machinima:** a method of making animated film using software similar to that designed for making video and computer games.

> **Demoscene:** a computer art subculture that specializes in producing audio-visual presentations (demos) that run in real-time on a computer. The main goal of a demo is to show off programming, artistic, and musical skills.

Popular social media icons

and government agencies alike use social media networks for rapid communication with friends and family, constituents, residents, current clients, and prospective customers. Let's first take a look at the global landscape and then hone in on social media trends in the United States. Table 6.1 notes the number of monthly active users (MAUs) globally and their usage of social media sites—Facebook, YouTube, and WhatsApp ranked among the top worldwide. Global social media networks are available in multiple languages and display strong user engagement (Clement, 2020) from their two billion Internet users that represent 25% of the world's population. Some platforms facilitate the exchange of messages, images, and videos between family and friends while others promote status sharing and social games.

Perrin and Anderson (2019) at the Pew Research Center assert that the United States demonstrates preferences that differ slightly from global trends, particularly among the adult population. Outside of YouTube and Facebook which rank similarly at the top, Americans enjoy specialized platforms like LinkedIn that provide a professional networking community that encourages the sharing of information, ideas, and career interests via a virtual forum. San Francisco-based Twitter, a microblogging service on which users post and interact with messages

TABLE 6.1 Global Social Networks Ranked by Number of Monthly Active Users

Ranking as of April 2020	Social Network	Monthly Active Users (MAUs)
1	Facebook	2.498 billion
2	YouTube	2.0 billion
3	WhatsApp	2.0 billion
4	Facebook Messenger	1.3 billion
5	Weixin/WeChat	1.165 billion
6	Instagram	1.0 billion
7	Douyin/TikTok	800 million
8	QQ	731 million
9	QZone	517 million
10	Sina Weibo	516 million

Source: Statista. Recreated by Jake Aguas.

known as "tweets," and visual discovery engines like Pinterest are currently more popular in the United States than in other countries.

The last few years have also seen an emergence in popularity of video instant messaging apps popular among teens and tweens who directly communicate through an app as opposed to phone calls and text messages. Video-sharing social networking service TikTok has 96 million users in the United States alone (Matsakis, 2019) and video walkie-talkie app, Marco Polo, is growing in usage.

Web 3.0, the "semantic web," is now contextualizing and managing trillions of web pages, whereas Google effectively functions with millions. Web 3.0 is a paradigm that:

> **Web 3.0:** The third generation of the World Wide Web that focuses on using machine-based understanding of data to provide a data-driven and semantic web.

> will make people's online lives easier and more intuitive as smarter applications such as better search functions give users exactly what they are looking for since it will be akin to artificial intelligence which

FIGURE 6.2 Percentage of US Adults who say they ever use the following online platforms or messaging apps online or on their cell phone

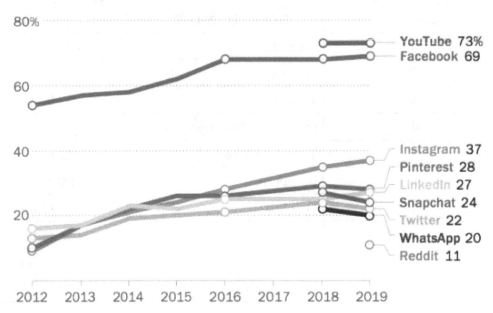

Source: Perrin, A., & Anderson, M. (2019, April 10). Share of the U.S. adults using social media, including Facebook, is mostly unchanged since 2018. Pew Research Center. Retrieved from https://www. pewresearch.org/fact-tank/2019/04/10/share-of-u-s-adults-using-social-media-including-facebook-is-mostly-unchanged-since-2018/

understands context rather than simply comparing keywords, as is currently the case (Technopedia, 2019).

Web 3.0 continues to narrow the communication gap between human web users and computerized applications—users are moving toward conduct-contextualized interactions with virtual assistants and search engines loaded with predetermined user behavior. Let me add some color to this thought. Today, if you typed "mustang," into any of the major search engines, the first few hundred results would yield news, images, and videos about the American muscle car. This result might serve you well if you were a muscle car enthusiast, but not a ceramic horse collector. Using algorithms, Web 3.0 will recognize your user behavior and present you with results based on your preferences and behavioral history. If you were an equine veterinarian, a search for "mustang" will predict that you are looking for information regarding the free-roaming horses of the American West and display customized results accordingly. In the same way, if you were a student preparing for a management knowledge contest sponsored by the Future Farmers of America, your results for "mustang" might return personalized results regarding the four phases of hippology: horse judging, written examination and slide identification, ID stations, and team problem solving. The point is that Web 3.0 will contextualize and customize your web experience by tailoring its relevant suggestions and recommendations.

Olivier Le Moal/Shutterstock.com

Future versions of the Web are the subject of deep discussion; however, there are some preliminary indicators showing us how it will be used. Web 4.0—the "symbiotic web," or "Web OS"—depicts the Web as being a single operating system, blurring the line between humans and machines. According to IGI Global (2020), Web 4.0 adds further sophistication and higher levels of intelligence and uses descriptives like autonomous, self-learning, collaboration, and content generation on mature semantic reasoning technologies and artificial intelligence. Spisak (2019) claims that Web 4.0 is occurring simultaneously with Web 3.0 and defines it more by its method of connection and accessibility than by its capabilities.

In this sense, the "mobile web" is connecting the world to more mobile devices and through more connections than there are people on the planet.

Web 5.0, the "emotional web" or "intelligent web" is more theoretical and conceptual at this point. Still, theorists predict that it will come sooner than later based on the rate of historical progress and advancements in technology. Virtual assistants predicting your needs from your behavioral patterns? Applications using algorithms to interpret information on complex levels, both emotionally and logically? Technology enabling computers to think in human fashion, detect subtleties, perceive emotions, reason, and respond with meaningful interactions is closer than we think, "true symbiosis with daily life, organically intertwined with what we do" (Spisak, 2019, p. 1).

Discussion Questions

1. Take a moment to recall your first memories and experiences with the World Wide Web and the Internet. What device(s) were you using? How specifically did you use the Web and the Internet? What types of applications/programs were you interacting with? What was their purpose?

2. Create a list of five distinct ways you use the Web and the Internet today. How has your usage (in weekly hours) changed over the last few years? What apps and programs do you use most often? How do they benefit you personally and professionally?

3. How has the emergence of home automation (smart home) and wireless car electronic computer systems shaped the way you manage your daily routine? Compare and contrast five benefits and limitations of these systems.

4. Conduct some additional research on Web 4.0. Identify five characteristics of Web 4.0 not yet discussed. In your opinion, have we arrived at Web 4.0? Explain three specific reasons why you have taken that position using the information that you have uncovered.

5. Overall, what are the three most significant changes that you have observed in the Web and the Internet in the last 5 to 10 years? Provide three examples and their implications.

References

Carsten P. (2013, November 27). Microsoft blocks censorship of Skype in China: Advocacy group. *NBC News.* Retrieved from https://www.nbcnews.com/technology/microsoft-blocks-censorship-skype-china-advocacy-group-2D11664965

Center for the Digital Future at USC Annenberg. (2018). *Surveying the digital future: The 16th annual study on the impact of digital technology on Americans.*

Retrieved from https://www.digitalcenter.org/wp-content/uploads/2018/12/2018-Digital-Future-Report.pdf

Clement, J. (2020, April 24). Global social networks ranked by number of users 2020. *Statista.* Retrieved from https://www.statista.com/statistics/272014/global-social-networks-ranked-by-number-of-users/

DiNucci, D. (1999). Fragmented future. *Print, 53*(4), 221–222.

Hosch, W. L. (2017). Web 2.0. *Encyclopedia Britannica.* Retrieved from https://www.britannica.com/topic/Web-20

IGI Global. (2020). *What is Web 4.0?* Retrieved from https://www.igi-global.com/dictionary/overview-differentiation-evolutionary-steps-web/35103

Liu, S. (2019, July 22). Mobile OS: Market share in Russia 2012–2019. *Statista.* Retrieved from https://www.statista.com/statistics/262174/market-share-held-by-mobile-operating-systems-in-russia/

Matsakis, L. (2019, March 6). A beginner's guide to TikTok. *Wired.* Retrieved from https://www.wired.com/story/how-to-use-tik-tok/

McPeak, A. (2018, January 24). A brief history of web browsers and how they work. *CrossBrowserTesting.* Retrieved from https://crossbrowsertesting.com/blog/test-automation/history-of-web-browsers/

Melkadze, A. (2019, September 18). Forecast of internet user numbers in Russia from 2015 to 2022. *Statista.* Retrieved from https://www.statista.com/statistics/567007/predicted-number-of-internet-users-in-russia/

Nix, E. (2018, August 30). The world's first web site. *History.com.* Retrieved from https://www.history.com/news/the-worlds-first-web-site

Perrin, A., & Anderson, M. (2019, April 10). Share of the U.S. adults using social media, including Facebook, is mostly unchanged since 2018. *Pew Research Center.* Retrieved from https://www.pewresearch.org/fact-tank/2019/04/10/share-of-u-s-adults-using-social-media-including-facebook-is-mostly-unchanged-since-2018/

Schwartz, E. (2014, August 6). 5 advantages to Yandex over Google in Russia. *SEMrush.* Retrieved from https://www.semrush.com/blog/5-advantages-yandex-google-russia/

Shontell, A. (2011, June 29). Flashback: This is what the first ever website looked like. *Business Insider.* Retrieved from https://www.businessinsider.com/flashback-this-is-what-the-first-website-ever-looked-like-2011-6

Spisak, K. (2019, September 13). Eras of the Web: Web 0.0 through 5.0. *Business 2 Community.* Retrieved from https://www.business2community.com/tech-gadgets/eras-of-the-web-web-0-0-through-web-5-0-02239654

Strickland, J. (2008, January 28). Is there a Web 1.0? *How Stuff Works.* Retrieved from https://computer.howstuffworks.com/web-101.htm

Sun, L. (2020, May 19). This Chinese search engine continues to grow in Baidu's shadow. *The Motley Fool.* Retrieved from https://www.fool.com/investing/2020/05/19/chinese-search-engine-sogou-grow-baidu-shadow.aspx

Technopedia. (2019, February 25). *What does Web 3.0 mean?* Retrieved from https://www.techopedia.com/definition/4923/web-30

Weber, L. (2011, July 13). Why do people use the internet? *Addictionblog.* Retrieved from https://internet.addictionblog.org/why-do-people-use-the-internet-10-reasons/